CHILD SEXUAL ABUSE IN THE CATHOLIC CHURCH

CHILD SEXUAL ABUSE IN THE CATHOLIC CHURCH

Other books in the At Issue series:

261.8

CHILD SEXUAL ABUSE IN THE CATHOLIC CHURCH

Louise I. Gerdes, *Book Editor*

Daniel Leone, *President*
Bonnie Szumski, *Publisher*
Scott Barbour, *Managing Editor*
Helen Cothran, *Senior Editor*

GREENHAVEN
PRESS®

San Diego • Detroit • New York • San Francisco • Cleveland
New Haven, Conn. • Waterville, Maine • London • Munich

© 2003 by Greenhaven Press. Greenhaven Press is an imprint of The Gale Group, Inc., a division of Thomson Learning, Inc.

Greenhaven® and Thomson Learning™ are trademarks used herein under license.

For more information, contact
Greenhaven Press
27500 Drake Rd.
Farmington Hills, MI 48331-3535
Or you can visit our Internet site at http://www.gale.com

LIBRARY OF CONGRESS CATALOGING-IN-PUBLICATION DATA
Child sexual abuse in the Catholic Church / Louise I. Gerdes, book editor.
p. cm. — (At issue)
Includes bibliographical references and index.
ISBN 0-7377-1803-X (alk. paper) — ISBN 0-7377-1804-8 (pbk. : alk. paper)
1. Child sexual abuse by clergy. 2. Catholic Church—Clergy—Sexual behavior.
I. Gerdes, Louise I. II. At issue (San Diego, Calif.)
BX1912.9.C47 2003
261.8'3272'08822—dc21   .   2002041630

Printed in the United States of America

Contents

Introduction

In 1984, the first year of his assignment to the Boston diocese, Cardinal Bernard Law approved the transfer of Father John J. Geoghan to St. Julia's parish in Weston, Massachusetts, despite substantial evidence that Geoghan had sexually abused children during previous assignments. Geoghan had been treated several times for molesting boys and had been removed from at least two parishes for sexually abusing children.

In 1989 Geoghan was forced to take sick leave after complaints that he was again sexually abusing children and, once again, he was treated and returned to the parish. Unfortunately, he continued to abuse children until 1993, when he was finally removed from parish duty. Since the mid-1990s, more than 130 people have come forward with allegations that the former priest fondled or raped them in incidences spanning three decades. However, not until 1998 did the church actually remove Geoghan from the priesthood. Finally, in February 2002, Geoghan was sentenced to ten years in prison for sexually abusing a ten-year-old boy.

Allegations of a cover-up by Cardinal Law and the Catholic Church did not become a national controversy, however, until January 6, 2002, when the *Boston Globe* ran the following headline on its front page: "Church Allowed Abuse by Priest for Years." In the months that followed, the national media reported a stream of cases that linked Catholic priests to child sexual abuse. By April 2002 at least 177 priests had been removed from their duties. One priest, Father Don Rooney, committed suicide after being accused of abusing a young female parishioner twenty-two years earlier. News reports also revealed that by the mid-1990s the church faced more than two hundred lawsuits concerning allegations of sexual abuse that cost the church $400 million in settlements, legal fees, and medical expenses for abuse victims.

In response to the scandal, Catholic officials denied allegations that they had attempted to hide child sexual abuse, and American bishops tried to depict the problem as one blown out of proportion by the media. According to Mark Chopko, general counsel of the U.S. Conference of Catholic Bishops, "There is no cover-up. People are confusing protecting the privacy of some individuals involved with the view that there's been persistent criminal conduct by the leadership of the church." However, outraged clergy and parishioners disagreed. According to Father Gary Hayes, president of the group Linkup: Survivors of Clergy Abuse and himself a victim of abuse by two priests while a teenager, "while individual bishops and dioceses have responded well to this crisis, the church as a whole has responded with arrogance, defiance, ignorance, and indifference . . . the real problem is that we have a hierarchy more interested in protecting its image than the innocence of its children."

What surprised most people was not that some priests sexually abused children, but that the church knew of patterns of child sexual abuse by some of its priests yet continued to allow these men access to children. Catholic clergy and laity alike began to question the way the church had historically handled cases of child sexual abuse. As the scandal began to unfold, further evidence emerged supporting the allegations that the American church hierarchy was at best ignorant of how to deal with child sexual abuse and at worst actively covering up the problem. The national media investigation that followed the exposé was the first time many Americans had heard about the extent of child sexual abuse in the Catholic Church. In fact, child sexual abuse had been occurring at least since the beginning of the twentieth century. (Many believe such abuse has been occurring throughout the history of the Catholic Church, but there is no evidence to substantiate these allegations.) Before the late 1970s, however, that fact was not generally known because church leaders managed clerical offenders discreetly, usually transferring them from their parishes without much publicity. Sometimes the church required that offending priests take a retreat or receive therapy, but priests were rarely reported to authorities or defrocked. Also during this time and into the 1980s, when parishioners complained to church leaders of child sexual abuse, they were often mistreated by church leaders, who often ignored or dealt with them as if somehow they had invited the abuse. In consequence, parishioners usually let the matter drop without taking further action. Not only did the church seem willing to conceal the problem from public view, the public appeared to be disinterested in the weaknesses, shortcomings, and even criminal behavior of religious leaders. Moreover, the media generally cooperated with the church in avoiding scandal.

However, public attitudes began to shift during the 1970s, a result of economic, social, and political changes. The women's movement, for example, brought new issues into the public eye; one of these issues was child sexual abuse. By the early 1980s, the civil courts began to hear cases alleging malpractice and negligence by respected professional groups and associations that did not effectively respond to allegations of child sexual abuse. In this new atmosphere, priests could be sued for the damages resulting from sexual liaisons with parishioners and the sexual abuse of children, and church leaders who were aware or should have been aware of these occurrences could be accused of negligence for permitting such behavior.

Criminal allegations against clergy also began to be brought in the 1980s. Before that time, priests, ministers, members of religious orders, and church workers had rarely been prosecuted in cases of child sexual abuse because neither victims nor church leaders reported such abuse to the authorities. However, the pervasive sexual abuse committed by Father Gilbert Gauthe in Lafayette, Louisiana, and the nationwide publicity that accompanied the scandal, resulted in church leaders being forced to report the more serious cases of child sexual abuse and gave some victims and their families the courage to pursue such cases on their own. Gauthe was suspected of molesting children as early as 1972. On several occasions, however, church authorities aware of his activities responded simply by moving him to new parishes where the molestations would recommence. Over twenty years, Gauthe molested up to one hundred boys in four parishes. In 1984 a number of parents of abused boys brought civil charges against the diocese over Gauthe's activities, and later that same year, the state filed criminal charges. Gauthe was sentenced to twenty years' imprisonment. In 1998 Gauthe won early parole for good conduct from a sympathetic Catholic judge. Unfortunately, within a few months he was arrested for molesting an underage boy and placed on probation.

The Gauthe scandal convinced many that church leaders had conducted a long-term cover-up of the sexual proclivities of some of its clergy. Media focus on a particular priest offender or on a particularly troubled diocese led to new allegations against other men or other church organizations in different parts of the country. The burgeoning number of sexual abuse scandals evoked deep concern among some Catholic observers, and in 1985 a confidential report entitled "The Problem of Sexual Molestation by Roman Catholic Clergy: Meeting the Problem in a Comprehensive and Responsible Manner" was submitted to the Catholic hierarchy. The authors were Gauthe's attorney, Ray Mouton, and two priests, Thomas P. Doyle and Michael R. Peterson. Doyle was a canon lawyer working at the Vatican embassy in Washington, D.C., and Peterson was the founder of St. Luke's Institute, which provided therapy for sexually troubled priests. In view of the escalating scandal and the multimillion-dollar legal actions, all three urged Catholic leaders to take strong and effective action to deal with the impending crisis.

In the autumn of 1985, U.S. bishops discussed the report in secret sessions at their semiannual gathering. However, the bishops would only commit to deal with cases of child sexual abuse as they arose in each diocese. Creating a nationwide church policy on child sexual abuse, the bishops believed, ran against the essential autonomy of each bishop in his diocese. When Doyle spoke publicly about the report and the problem of clergy child sexual abuse, many bishops were offended, and Doyle's career as a Vatican representative ended.

The American clergy sexual abuse problem was subsumed by a new wave of scandals, which broke outside the United States. Clergy child sexual abuse scandals emerged in Australia, Austria, Canada, Ireland, and Italy. In the spring of 1989, for example, in the province of Newfoundland in Canada, attention shifted to physical and sexual abuse committed by members of the Christian Brothers Congregation against teenage boys in the Mount Cashel boys home in Saint John's. In this case, allegations had originally surfaced in 1975, and in a widespread state-church cover-up, certain brothers had been permitted to leave the province without facing criminal proceedings. The story remained in the headlines for several years.

By the 1990s the public was learning that it was not only possible, but also commonplace for Catholic priests, officially celibate, to be sexually active, and for church officials to turn a blind eye when revelations of child sexual abuse came to the surface. Despite the public's outrage, the 1985 report to American bishops, and growing evidence that some Catholic clergy were sexually active, American Catholic Church leaders continued to deal with clergy child sexual abuse as it had for decades and failed to develop a formal response to the clergy child sexual abuse problem.

Commentators offer a number of reasons why the Catholic Church hierarchy failed to implement effective policies to deal with child sexual abuse. Some contend that because the church views sexual offences as moral failures, it takes the position that if offenders repent, they should be forgiven and provided counseling. Once rehabilitated, offenders should then be transferred to another position. Unfortunately, many observers argue, this philosophy kept church leaders ignorant of the fact that sexual abuse can quickly become compulsive—it cannot be assumed that even with extensive therapy priests will never abuse again. Many experts claim that abusing priests must be prohibited from all contact with minors. For some this means defrocking offending priests; for others it means removing them from duties that would bring them into contact with children.

Other analysts argue that church officials are only concerned with the good name of the church and avoiding or limiting legal liability for the harm done to victims. Church officials, these analysts argue, confuse loyalty to the institutional church and its ministers with loyalty to the people of God. According to Laurie Goodstein, a columnist for the *New York Times*, when the *Boston Globe* reported the clergy abuse scandal in the Boston diocese in January 2002, the bishops "behaved more like Senators or CEOs engaged in damage control than as moral teachers engaged in the gospel." Observers such as Goodstein maintain that to avoid accountability, the hierarchy of the Catholic Church shifts blame for the child sexual abuse crisis to other issues. Church officials, they claim, blame the secular press, homosexuality in the priesthood, and the sexual revolution of the 1960s and 1970s rather than take action to address the problem. To solve the child sexual abuse problem, many analysts maintain, the hierarchy must emphasize compassion for victims over protection of the church's image.

Another reason why child sexual abuse flourished within the church is that there is too little oversight over the bishops, who have too much power, according to many commentators. Nobel Peace Prize–winning cardiologist James E. Muller claims that "the core of the [child sexual abuse] problem is centralized power, with no voice of the faithful." Some suggest that one change the church hierarchy could make to help prevent future child sexual abuse problems would be to give the laity more say in church policies. Muller argues for a lay power structure at the local, national, and global level to represent the voice of the 1 billion Catholic lay people in discussions with parish priests, bishops, and the pope.

Unfortunately, after years of obeisance to church authority, many Catholics find it difficult to express their dissatisfaction with the response of the church hierarchy to the crisis of clergy child sexual abuse. Former Massachusetts Lieutenant Governor Thomas P. O'Neill Jr., son of the late U.S. House Speaker "Tip" O'Neill, says he had struggled with his own fear when he left his position as Cardinal Law's adviser to become a supporter of Voice of the Faithful, a lay reform group founded in February 2002 in response to the child sexual abuse scandal. "I wasn't raised to be the kind of Catholic who tells bishops or popes something they might not want to hear," said O'Neill. "But all that made the abuse and the cover-up possible must change in this church. I don't think anything else will do."

People continue to debate whether the Catholic Church has done enough to protect children from clergy who sexually abuse children and whether the laity should have a greater voice in church policy on this and other matters. The authors in *At Issue: Child Sexual Abuse in the Catholic Church* offer several perspectives on the nature and scope of the problem of clergy child sexual abuse as well as possible solutions.

1

Child Sexual Abuse in the Catholic Church: An Overview

Kenneth Jost

Kenneth Jost, a staff writer for the CQ Researcher, *contributes to the* American Bar Association Journal *and is adjunct professor at Georgetown University Law Center.*

Media coverage linking Catholic priests to reports of pedophilia set off an international debate over the causes and consequences of child sexual abuse in the Catholic Church. For example, while some Catholics blame the church hierarchy for failing to protect their children from sexual abuse, others believe the church acted in good faith when dealing with reports of sexual abuse by priests. Church representatives, victims' organizations, former priests, child abuse scholars, and other authorities hold different positions on several questions, including whether priests accused of child sexual abuse should be prosecuted or treated, whether the discipline of celibacy contributes to child sexual abuse, and whether homosexuals should be allowed into the priesthood.

G reg Ford radiated playful energy and innocence as a preschooler in suburban Newton, Massachusetts. But sometime after age 6—for no apparent reason—Ford developed behavior problems. By his teen years, they had worsened into drug and alcohol abuse and suicide attempts.

A predator is revealed

Now his parents think they know why. Amid national media coverage of sexual abuse by Roman Catholic priests, Ford, at 24, told his parents for the first time that the pastor of his neighborhood church had molested him repeatedly for five years.

By Ford's account, the Reverend Paul Shanley introduced him to sexual activity that began with undressing and continued to masturbation

Kenneth Jost, "Sexual Abuse and the Clergy," *CQ Researcher*, vol. 12, May 3, 2002, pp. 395–402.

and anal sex—all before he became a teenager. More shocking to the Fords, files from the Archdiocese of Boston now show that church officials knew of numerous accusations of abuse by Shanley dating back to 1966, just six years after his ordination as a priest, but continued to put him in positions involving contact with young children.

"I am very upset that a lot of people knew about him and what he was doing," Ford told an April 8, 2002, news conference called in connection with the civil damage suit he filed in February 2002 against the head of the Boston Archdiocese, Cardinal Bernard Law, for allegedly covering up years of abuse by Shanley.

Ford says Shanley molested "hundreds" of children in Newton and elsewhere. "I hope he rots in hell," he concluded.

Shanley, a once-popular "street priest," 70 years old in May 2002, belatedly had admitted in 1993 to molesting nine boys, according to church documents released by Ford. But Shanley is nowhere to be found. The outspokenly gay priest was last seen in California, where he operated a gay resort in Palm Springs. [Shanley is living in Provincetown, Massachusetts, awaiting trial.]

> *A substantial majority of Catholics—in Boston and around the country—believe the church has mishandled accusations of sexual abuse by priests.*

Law himself fought a losing court battle to keep Shanley's files under wraps and then issued, through an aide, what most considered a weak apology for mishandling the case. The archdiocese "has learned from the painful experience of the inadequate policies and procedures of the past," said Donna Morrissey, Law's spokeswoman. Without specifically referring to the documents, Morrissey added: "Whatever may have occurred in the past, there were no deliberate decisions to put children at risk."

Shanley's case represented the third mortification in just four months for church officials in heavily Catholic Boston. In January 2002, *The Boston Globe* reported that the archdiocese also had known of abuse accusations against the now-defrocked John Geoghan, while continuing to give him pastoral assignments for a period of years. Then in April 2002, the newspaper revealed that the archdiocese also had failed to take decisive action against the Reverend Joseph Birmingham, despite receiving substantial accusations from parents in two of the Massachusetts parishes he served prior to his death in 1989.

A crisis of trust

The *Globe's* coverage touched off a wrenching debate across the country about an issue that had surfaced before, but never so intensively or so painfully. Newspapers, magazines and television news programs carried an unceasing stream of stories linking Catholic priests in more than a dozen communities to pedophilia—sexual activity with children below the age of puberty—or sexual abuse of older youngsters.

The disclosures elicited torrents of criticism from Catholics across the ideological spectrum. "This is the greatest crisis in the modern history of the Catholic Church," says the Reverend Richard McBrien, a prominent and outspokenly liberal professor of theology at the University of Notre Dame in Indiana. "It raises serious questions about the integrity of its priesthood, and the Catholic Church just can't function without a priesthood that has the support and trust of its people."

William Donohue, a conservative Catholic who heads the Catholic League for Religious and Civil Rights, uses even stronger language. "I don't know of a single Catholic priest or layman who isn't furious about the sex-abuse scandal, in terms of the tolerance [the hierarchy] has had for intolerable behavior and the way they've played musical chairs with these miscreant priests," Donohue says. "I've never seen such anger."

Further fueling that anger were revelations that over the years the church had paid tens of millions of dollars in settlements to victims, often stipulating that they not discuss the cases.

Debating the church's response

In vain, a few Catholic leaders have tried to dispel the impression that church officials actively tried to bury the scandal. "It's never been a secret or an attempt to keep it secret," says Mark Chopko, general counsel of the U.S. Conference of Catholic Bishops, whose members include the bishops of the country's 195 Catholic dioceses. "There is no cover-up. People are confusing protecting the privacy of some individuals involved with the view that there's been persistent criminal conduct by the leadership of the church. That's not my experience over the past 15 years."

Nonetheless, poll after poll shows that a substantial majority of Catholics—in Boston and around the country—believe the church has mishandled accusations of sexual abuse by priests. In Boston, a substantial majority of Catholics also have told pollsters they want Law to resign as head of the archdiocese. He has refused. [Law resigned in December 2002.]

Catholic leaders today stand condemned for failing to refer priests accused of sexual abuse for criminal prosecution and instead seeking to rehabilitate them.

Groups representing victims of clerical abuse say they welcome the new attention to issues they have been raising for more than a decade. But they also say they are still dissatisfied with the Catholic hierarchy's response.

"Some bishops have come forward and given names to prosecutors and have been out front on the issue," according to the Reverend Gary Hayes, a Catholic priest in Cloverport, Kentucky, and president of the group Linkup: Survivors of Clergy Abuse. "But the church as a whole has responded with arrogance, defiance, ignorance and indifference."

After initially resisting pressure to get involved, Pope John Paul II took the extraordinary step in April 2002 of summoning all U.S. cardinals to the Vatican in Rome to discuss the issue. The two-day meeting on April 23–24 ended with a communiqué promising the removal of "serial" child abusers as priests but stopping short of the zero-tolerance, "one-strike-and-you're-out" policy demanded by many victims' advocates.

For the country's 60 million Catholics, the sex-abuse scandals added controversy to persistent divisions among rank-and-file believers and between a somewhat liberal-leaning laity and a more conservative church hierarchy in the United States and Rome. Most American Catholics, for example, favor changing the centuries-old policies against allowing priests to marry and ordaining female priests—policies that could relieve the church's growing priest shortage, but that John Paul reaffirmed on the eve of his meeting with the U.S. cardinals. In addition, the controversy has raised questions about how to reconcile the apparent increase in the number of gay priests with the church's official prohibitions against homosexual conduct.

In light of the current scandal, other denominations are re-examining their policies toward sexual abuse by clergy. Some appeared to be fortifying existing policies to prevent misconduct, while others said they had few reported cases.

Similar scandals have hit the Catholic Church in other countries. A popular Catholic bishop in southeastern Ireland, Brendan Comiskey, resigned on April 1, 2002, expressing regret for failing to take stronger steps to deal with a priest who sexually assaulted dozens of boys in the 1980s and '90s. In the pope's native Poland, Archbishop Julius Paetz of Poznan resigned in March after an investigation showed a long history of sexual advances to teenage seminarians.

As the issues continue to roil within and beyond the Catholic Church, here are some of the major questions being debated:

Should clergy be prosecuted in cases of sexual abuse of minors?

Catholic leaders today stand condemned for failing to refer priests accused of sexual abuse for criminal prosecution and instead seeking to rehabilitate them through counseling and sometimes psychological treatment—returning many of them to pastoral positions. Hardly anyone defends that practice any longer, but Catholic officials and supportive laypersons insist the church leaders acted in good faith and in accord with a once-prevailing consensus among child-abuse experts.

"The cases that are being written about in Boston and around the country are cases that came up 20 to 30 years ago and were dealt with under the conventional social standards of the time," says Chopko. "It was thought that one shouldn't make such a big deal of this because it would just traumatize people later. And there was in the therapeutic community the illusion that the people who do this are curable."

"I'm not going to sit here and make excuses for what went on 20 years ago," Chopko adds. "But we're seeing what happened in dioceses before there were policies in place and before we had the best information" about how to deal with abuse cases.

"The bishops followed their conscience in a way that turned out to be not correct," says the Reverend John McCloskey, director of the Washington-based Catholic Information Center. "It's pretty clear from here on in that that will not be the case."

Victims' advocates are less forgiving of what the Reverend Hayes—who says he was abused by two priests while a teenager—calls the "unconscionable" policies of the past. "The leadership of the church has lied about these things, has covered up these things, has transferred priests from parish to parish, diocese to diocese, and given clean bills of health to these guys when they know they've done these things," he says.

But the victims' advocacy groups welcome the church's promise now to refer future cases to law enforcement authorities. "We are finally beginning to see secular authorities beginning to treat the church just as any other institution, with no special deference or privileges," says David Clohessy, national director of the Survivors Network of those Abused by Priests (SNAP).

Should priests receive treatment?

Still, both Hayes and Clohessy say priests should also be given treatment. "These are sick people," Hayes says. "They are not evil people as the hierarchy has tried to portray them. They have a disease."

"If they can find treatment and help for their condition, wonderful—but not as an alternative to prosecution. They should go hand in hand."

Psychologists and psychotherapists who have worked with priest abuse cases now play down the possibility of "curing" people who are sexually attracted to young children. Many pedophiles were sexually abused themselves as children. Some research also indicates a possible biological cause.

"True pedophiles cannot be treated well enough to be returned to a pastoral role," says Gary Schoener, a clinical psychologist in Minneapolis who has worked with victims of clergy sexual abuse. "You can never treat them well enough to make them safe to return to the pulpit."

"They deserve consideration, they deserve compassion, they deserve treatment," says Frederick Berlin, an associate professor of psychiatry at Johns Hopkins University Medical School in Baltimore and founder of its Sexual Disorders Clinic. Still, Berlin says, "once [an offender] has crossed the border into sexual behavior with minors, he's in the criminal arena."

Psychologists . . . warn that celibacy may contribute to the clerical sexual-abuse problem by attracting sexually immature or confused men to the priesthood.

While many of the recent cases have involved pedophilia, many others—perhaps most—have involved teenagers. The condition has been labeled ephebephilia: an inordinate sexual attraction by adult males to young boys. These cases are "more treatable," according to the Reverend Stephen J. Rossetti, president of St. Luke Institute, a Catholic psychiatric hospital in Silver Spring, Maryland, just outside Washington, that treats priests with sexual disorders.

Rossetti, a clinical psychologist, concedes that bishops made "serious errors" in handling cases in the past. "They became judge, jury and parole officer, and that's not their role," he says. In the future, he calls for closer cooperation between church and law enforcement authorities. But he also calls for treating offenders. "We can't ignore them," Rossetti says "or else they will go on being perpetrators."

Berlin, who is a member of a study commission created by Cardinal Law to deal with the issue, agrees. "If all we do is send a person with pedophilia to prison, it's important to realize that nothing in prison is going to erase this," Berlin says. "Looking at what's best for the community, if we are going to put people into prison, it's important to combine prison with some form of treatment. This is a criminal-justice matter and a public health matter."

Should the Catholic Church make celibacy optional for priests?

For more than a decade, the American Catholic Church has been suffering a pronounced shortage of priests. Thousands have left the priesthood, while enrollments at seminaries have dropped sharply. The most frequently offered explanation is the church's mandatory policy of requiring priests to abstain from any form of sexual activity—in or out of marriage, heterosexual or homosexual.

The current sex-abuse crisis seems to some critics both in and out of the church as one more reason for abandoning a practice with uncertain doctrinal origins and seemingly out of touch with modern views of human sexuality.

"Why put such a restriction on such an important ministry, particularly when there's a precipitous decline in the number of people who present themselves for the priesthood?" asks McBrien at Notre Dame.

Catholic officials, however, say the celibacy issue is unrelated to the recent disclosures of sexual abuse by priests. "Most people who abuse children are married," says Chopko, of the Conference of Bishops. "You're not dealing with a problem that is related to celibacy. To an extent, it's a red herring. It's a fake issue."

"The scandals exposed in recent months have not been 'caused' by celibacy," says George Weigel, the pope's biographer and a prominent lay Catholic who is a senior fellow at the Ethics and Public Policy Center in Washington. "They have been caused by men who have failed to live the solemn, celibate commitment they made. A man given to sexual predation is just as likely to be a sexual predator if he's married."

Victims' advocates and other critics, however, say celibacy plays an important part in the sexual-abuse crisis by fostering what they call "a culture of secrecy."

"In a group where nobody is allowed to have sex, then many priests have secrets," SNAP's Clohessy says. "And that makes it tougher for them to report other priests involved in misconduct."

"The institutional flaw responsible for the church's behavior is that you never break silence against another priest, especially in sexual matters," says Mark Jordan, a professor of religion at Emory University in Atlanta and an openly gay Catholic. "That rule of secrecy is directly linked to the culture of priestly celibacy. In order to maintain the facade of celibacy, you have to create a system for keeping secrets."

Psychologists also warn that celibacy may contribute to the clerical sexual-abuse problem by attracting sexually immature or confused men to the priesthood. "There may be some sexually disordered people who have naively convinced themselves that by being a priest they are going to solve their problems," Berlin of Johns Hopkins says.

While experts agree that celibacy has no correlation with pedophilia, Schoener says it may be a factor in some of the cases of sexual contact between priests and teenagers. "Celibacy plays a role with some of the ephebephiles," Schoener says. "Some people are not equipped to handle these impulses because they've not been through adolescent dating, because they've not dated women or, among gay priests, because they've not dated men."

Supporters of celibacy say it concentrates priests' time and energy on their pastoral responsibilities. "It's been highly successful in having people dedicate themselves" to the church, the Catholic Information Center's McCloskey says. The defenders also say that the church is doing a better job today than in the past of screening candidates for the priesthood for potential sexual issues. "Our seminaries are getting more screening—in terms of sexuality—than any other profession," Rossetti says.

Still, critics point out that the Catholic Church's policy on celibacy is neither universal nor uniform. Priests in the Eastern Orthodox Christian churches are not required to remain celibate, nor are Protestant ministers. And the Catholic Church permits married Episcopalian priests who convert to Catholicism to remain married.

For his part, Richard Sipe, a psychotherapist and former monk who favors making celibacy optional, says it can be a valuable practice for some priests. "Celibacy will always endure. It is a part of nature for some people," says Sipe, who has written several books on the subject. "But I don't believe you can require it of somebody. That's an internal discovery. It's something that comes from inside."

Whatever views American Catholics have on celibacy, any change will have to come from the Vatican, which has actively discouraged any discussion of the issue. "There's not really much the American church can do," says Philip Jenkins, a professor of religious studies at Pennsylvania State University and a former Catholic who is now Episcopalian. "The chance that the church overall is giving to change celibacy is very small."

"There are arguments on both sides," he adds, "But if they do it, they should do it for the right reason, not as a response to a crisis."

Should gay men be barred from the priesthood?

When the Rev. George Spagnolia faced a 30-year-old accusation of sexual molestation, the popular Lowell, Massachusetts, priest also had to confront a second issue: his homosexuality. "Being gay doesn't mean you're a pedophile," Spagnolia told a March 1, 2002, news conference. "I'm saying, 'Yes, I've had gay relationships.' But I've never harmed a child."

Spagnolia's denial of the accusation that he molested a 14-year-old Boston boy on two occasions in 1971 did not prevent Cardinal Law from placing him on administrative leave as pastor of the St. Patrick's parish. And although Spagnolia insists there is no connection between homosexuality and sexual abuse, the current scandal over pedophilia among the clergy has prompted prominent Catholics—including the Vatican it-self—to question whether gay men should be barred from the priesthood.

"People with these inclinations just cannot be ordained," Dr. Joaquin Navarro-Valls, Pope John Paul II's spokesman, told *The New York Times* in early March 2002. "That does not imply a final judgment on people with homosexuality," he added. "But you cannot be in this field."

The statement from Navarro-Valls—a Spanish layman trained as a psychiatrist—provoked disbelief among many U.S. Catholics and outright anger from gay Catholics. "This is nothing more than a vicious and transparent attempt to shift the blame," Mary Louise Cervone, president of the gay Catholic group Dignity/USA, said in a statement the next day.

The current scandal over pedophilia among the clergy has prompted prominent Catholics . . . to question whether gay men should be barred from the priesthood.

Leaders of the two major victims'-advocacy groups also criticize Navarro-Valls' statement. "Some members of the hierarchy and even the Vatican are trying to use the homosexual issue as a way to scapegoat [gay] priests and a way to avoid talking about the real problems," Linkup's Hayes says. "[Both] heterosexual and homosexual men abuse children. We need to talk about why men abuse children."

Still, the dispute has highlighted the fact that the Catholic priesthood includes many gay men—even though the church officially teaches that homosexuality is a disorder and homosexual conduct a sin. The proportion of gay priests in the United States has been variously estimated at anywhere from 2 percent to 50 percent. A random nationwide survey of priests in 1999 by the *Kansas City Star* found that 15 percent of respondents identified themselves as gay and another 5 percent as bisexual.

Whatever the exact percentage, it has almost certainly risen sharply in the past two decades, in part because of the exodus of many heterosexual priests to marry. Conservative Catholics, including members of the traditionalist Opus Dei movement, view the apparent increase as reason to take overt steps to bar, or at least limit, the ordination of gay men.

"They are promiscuous and have proven to be promiscuous," says the Catholic Information Center's McCloskey, a member of Opus Dei. "I don't think the Catholic Church can countenance having people in the priesthood who have what, in Catholic eyes, is a disorder."

"Gays have a very difficult time living chastely," says author Weigel of the Ethics and Public Policy Center—quoting as an authority Andrew Sullivan, the conservative journalist-author and openly gay Catholic. "If that's true, then it seems to me that the church ought to be very, very careful about ordaining gay men. I would say the exact same thing about ordaining heterosexuals who have shown an inability to live chaste lives."

The extent of sexual activity between priests is uncertain. Cervone says sexually active gay priests typically do not have other priests as partners. But Sipe, who based a 1990 book on celibacy on surveys of hundreds of priests, says a "network of sexually active priests" exists in the church.

Emory University's Jordan says gay sexual activity has been part of seminary life for centuries, despite the church's explicit efforts in recent decades to weed out homosexuals. "Catholic seminaries became for many gay men places of sexual self-discovery," he writes.

Psychologists minimize, somewhat, the link between homosexuality and sexual abuse. "There is no evidence whatsoever that pedophilia occurs more frequently among homosexuals" than among heterosexuals, Berlin says, while acknowledging that homosexuality may be related to some of the cases involving priests and older teens. "Some of this has been about homosexual men giving in to temptation with adolescent males," he says. Overall, though, "homosexuals are no more risk to children than heterosexuals."

Officially, U.S. bishops apparently want to steer clear of the issue of ordaining gay priests. "This is one of those side issues," says Chopko, of the bishops' conference. "We're not looking for people who are oriented one way or the other. We're looking for people who are oriented and properly disposed to living celibate chastity." He calls Navarro-Valls' statement "a throwaway line . . . a one-liner in a much longer interview."

For his part, Jordan says eliminating gay priests would be both self-destructive and impractical. "If you could fire all the gay priests tomorrow, you would so greatly reduce the number of priests that the church could no longer function," he says, adding that many of the gay men going into seminary "are so much into denial about their sexuality that I don't see how you could tell."

2

A Message from the Pope on the Child Sexual Abuse Crisis

John Paul II

John Paul II, the leader of the Catholic Church, was born Karol Jozef Wojtyla in Poland. Following the sudden death of Pope John Paul I in 1978, Wojtyla was elected as the first non-Italian pope in more than 450 years. He resides in the Vatican in Rome and is known as a pillar of moral conservatism for the Catholic Church.

The sexual abuse of children by some priests is not only a crime against society but also a sin in the eyes of God. It must be remembered, however, that the vast majority of priests continue to do great work. Child sexual abuse is a symptom of a crisis of sexual morality in society generally, so church leaders must clearly address this deep-seated crisis. Church leaders must inspire trust, effectively preach the gospel of Jesus Christ, and guide the faithful to God for healing to purify the Catholic Church and lead to a holier priesthood.

Editor's note: In April 2002, thirteen U.S. cardinals arrived in Vatican City to discuss ways to restore trust in the Catholic Church in the wake of child sexual abuse scandals occurring in the United States. On Tuesday, April 23, 2002, the pope delivered the following address to the U.S. cardinals.

Dear Brothers,
Let me assure you first of all that I greatly appreciate the effort you are making to keep the Holy See [the Vatican], and me personally, informed regarding the complex and difficult situation which has arisen in your country in early 2002. I am confident that your discussions here will bear much fruit for the good of the Catholic people of the United States. You have come to the house of the Successor of Peter [the Pope], whose task it is to confirm his brother Bishops in faith and love, and to unite them around

Christ in the service of God's People. The door of this house is always open to you. All the more so when your communities are in distress.

Like you, I too have been deeply grieved by the fact that priests and religious, whose vocation it is to help people live holy lives in the sight of God, have themselves caused such suffering and scandal to the young. Because of the great harm done by some priests and religious, the Church herself is viewed with distrust, and many are offended at the way in which the Church's leaders are perceived to have acted in this matter. The abuse which has caused this crisis is by every standard wrong and rightly considered a crime by society; it is also an appalling sin in the eyes of God. To the victims and their families, wherever they may be, I express my profound sense of solidarity and concern.

Promoting Christian values

It is true that a generalized lack of knowledge of the nature of the problem and also at times the advice of clinical experts led Bishops to make decisions which subsequent events showed to be wrong. You are working to establish more reliable criteria to ensure that such mistakes are not repeated. At the same time, even while recognizing how indispensable these criteria are, we cannot forget the power of Christian conversion, that radical decision to turn away from sin and back to God, which reaches to the depths of a person's soul and can work extraordinary change.

Neither should we forget the immense spiritual, human and social good that the vast majority of priests and religious in the United States have done and are still doing. The Catholic Church in your country has always promoted human and Christian values with great vigor and generosity, in a way that has helped to consolidate all that is noble in the American people.

The abuse which has caused this crisis is . . . rightly considered a crime by society; it is also an appalling sin in the eyes of God.

A great work of art may be blemished, but its beauty remains; and this is a truth which any intellectually honest critic will recognize. To the Catholic communities in the United States, to their Pastors and members, to the men and women religious, to teachers in Catholic universities and schools, to American missionaries in all parts of the world, go the wholehearted thanks of the entire Catholic Church and the personal thanks of the Bishop of Rome.

The abuse of the young is a grave symptom of a crisis affecting not only the Church but society as a whole. It is a deep-seated crisis of sexual morality, even of human relationships, and its prime victims are the family and the young. In addressing the problem of abuse with clarity and determination, the Church will help society to understand and deal with the crisis in its midst.

It must be absolutely clear to the Catholic faithful, and to the wider community, that Bishops and superiors are concerned, above all else, with the spiritual good of souls. People need to know that there is no place in the priesthood and religious life for those who would harm the young. They must know that Bishops and priests are totally committed to the fullness of Catholic truth on matters of sexual morality, a truth as essential to the renewal of the priesthood and the episcopate as it is to the renewal of marriage and family life.

We must be confident that this time of trial will bring a purification of the entire Catholic community, a purification that is urgently needed if the Church is to preach more effectively the Gospel of Jesus Christ in all its liberating force. Now you must ensure that where sin increased, grace will all the more abound (cf. Rom 5:20). So much pain, so much sorrow must lead to a holier priesthood, a holier episcopate, and a holier Church.

God alone is the source of holiness, and it is to Him above all that we must turn for forgiveness, for healing and for the grace to meet this challenge with uncompromising courage and harmony of purpose. Like the Good Shepherd of last Sunday's Gospel, Pastors must go among their priests and people as men who inspire deep trust and lead them to restful waters (cf. Ps 22:2).

I beg the Lord to give the Bishops of the United States the strength to build their response to the present crisis upon the solid foundations of faith and upon genuine pastoral charity for the victims, as well as for the priests and the entire Catholic community in your country. And I ask Catholics to stay close to their priests and Bishops, and to support them with their prayers at this difficult time.

The peace of the Risen Christ be with you!

3

Three Types of Child Sexual Abuse in the Catholic Church

William Rusher

William Rusher, a leading voice of the American right, was publisher of the National Review *from 1957 to 1988 and is a senior fellow of the Claremont Institute for the Study of Statesmanship and Political Philosophy, in Minneapolis, Minnesota.*

The child sexual abuse problem in the Catholic Church is actually comprised of three different problems requiring different solutions. One, priestly misbehavior with girls and women may require the church to rescind its celibacy requirement. Two, clergy misconduct with men and boys may require the church to ban homosexuals from the priesthood, or at least warn them about indulging in their desires. Three, since research shows that few true pedophiles can be "cured," pedophile priests should be prosecuted, and if prosecution is not possible, they should be kept away from children. However, if a priest has consensual sex with a young person who has reached the age of consent, he should be given the opportunity to reform.

The crisis in the Catholic Church over the sexual misbehavior of a small fraction of its priests has predictably been worsened by the latent hostility of much of the media. When the Justice Department announced the arrest of more than 100 men for participating in a child pornography ring on the Internet, every account that I saw or heard reported breathlessly that among those arrested were "six clergymen, including two Catholic priests." Imagine the uproar if they had been described as "six clergymen, including a Presbyterian minister and two rabbis."

But some remarkably sloppy thinking and talking on the part of both the media and the Church itself also worsen the problem. There are really three quite separate problems here, requiring quite different solutions.

First, there is the problem of priestly misbehavior with post-pubescent

William Rusher, "The Catholic Church's Three Problems," *Conservative Chronicle*, vol. 17, April 3, 2002, p. 23. Copyright © 2002 by United Media Enterprises. Reproduced by permission.

girls and women. No doubt the requirement of priestly celibacy imposes greater demands on certain heterosexual priests than they are ultimately able, or at any rate willing, to bear. This fact has been seized on to justify demands that the Catholic clergy be allowed to marry. That might well help solve this particular problem, but it clearly has no application to the second and third problems, discussed below. (I may add that I have long felt that the celibacy requirement has had devastating consequences for the Catholic gene pool, since for nearly two millennia it forbade some of the most talented males in each generation to reproduce, while rabbis, for example, were embracing fatherhood enthusiastically.)

These three [child sexual abuse] problems are quite different, and might well be treated differently by the ecclesiastical authorities.

Then there is the problem of priestly misbehavior with post-pubescent boys and men. It may well be true that a religious vocation is tempting to many homosexuals raised as Catholics, since obligatory celibacy eliminates pressures to marry and may also help them resist their desires. But, as with heterosexual priests, a small fraction will succumb to temptation. Insofar as there is any solution to this problem, it rests in stricter evaluation of postulants by the Church, to avoid ordaining homosexuals in the first place, or to recognize their proclivities and warn them about indulging them, rather than permit the Church to become a convenient screen for such behavior.

A different problem

Finally there is the problem of those priests who are genuine pedophiles—that is to say, who are sexually attracted to pre-pubescent girls or boys. Priests, and clergymen more generally, occupy positions of authority in their communities that make such despicable abuse relatively easy to commit and to cover up. Moreover, there is considerable evidence that this proclivity is extremely difficult to "cure." Those afflicted with it, therefore, are very likely to keep on with such abuse, even when discovered, unless they are forcibly prevented from doing so. For them, accordingly, the solution must be draconian: Prison for their crimes, or, if the statute of limitations has run, relocation where there is no opportunity to abuse children.

It should be obvious that these three problems are quite different, and might well be treated differently by the ecclesiastical authorities—normally, in the case of the Catholic Church, the local bishop. In the case of pedophiles, there must be no waffling: immediate suspension, and a prompt and public referral to the civilian legal authorities. Similarly, in the case of sexual misconduct with a post-pubescent girl or boy who has not reached the age of consent, a church has no option but to obey the laws of the jurisdiction.

But what if the youngster had reached the age of consent, and the sexual activity was consensual (and thus not unlawful) and was confined to a single episode, and the priest admits and repents it and gives convincing evidence of a determination to reform? I can well imagine that a bishop, with his lifelong commitment to the concepts of sin, confession, repentance and redemption, would favor forgiveness. And I would be hard put to say he was wrong.

I might add that, in all cases save the last, the ecclesiastical authorities must eschew any attempt at concealment. Such efforts merely simplify the task of those whose real purpose is to undermine the Church.

4

The Celibacy Requirement for Priests Contributes to Child Sexual Abuse

Eugene Kennedy

Eugene Kennedy is a professor of psychology at Loyola University in Chicago and author of the book The Unhealed Wound: The Church and Human Sexuality.

Not unlike the choice to marry, the reasons for choosing a celibate life may be unhealthy. Research shows that many priests do not view celibacy as a virtue that they voluntarily choose but as a condition to which they must adjust. Unfortunately, immature candidates for the priesthood are not yet aware of their own sexuality and may later become confused and tortured by sexual feelings that arise once they become priests. If a priest is particularly disturbed, he may act out his sexual conflict and sexually abuse the children in his care behind the shield of celibacy.

C elibacy is not in itself the cause of pedophilia in Catholic priests any more than marriage is the cause of divorce among married people. Both, however, are psychological states that only seem easy to understand. The motives people have for entering each state may not always be healthy, causing pain and heartache to more than the person making the choice.

Marriage appears so appropriate, so right, so to speak, for humans that it seems an almost natural institution. Yet marriage has been, and is, understood in almost contradictory ways across the cultures of the world. In some, it is a choice of the heart made by individuals, while in others, it is arranged by parents and therefore an act of obedience. To some, its only and overriding purpose is to stabilize the relationship in which children are born into the world. Others view it as ordered to the fulfillment and friendship that men and women seek so deeply in life.

The motives for marriage do not always match these varied ideals and the state may yield as much pain as it does happiness. The failure rate is high. And yet most people want to, and do, get married. Many of them learn, long after they have forgotten the words of their vows, that they never really knew either themselves or the person they married.

Understanding celibacy

Celibacy refers to an unmarried state. Chastity is something different: it applies to the unmarried and married alike, asking them to be faithful to a religious vow or to a spouse, respectively. Celibacy's history in the Roman Catholic Church is more of a discipline, as it is described, than a virtue, as it is promoted. It was introduced ten centuries after Jesus chose a married man to head his church, in order to prevent priests from handing on lands to their descendants.

While it can be understood as a voluntary choice made by people who want to give their whole lives in service to a community larger than their own family, it is, in practice, not free but a condition that must be accepted by young men who wish to be priests. During their training, the seminarians of years past typically learned of celibacy's possibilities of glory and the example of the saints who surrender marriage to serve the Lord.

[Celibacy] may, in some circumstances, incubate men who will lead tragic double lives behind its screen.

In reality, however, celibacy is a complex and subtle state. It may attract those aspiring to heroic virtue, but may also attract large numbers of persons with very different motivations. In a national study of American priests conducted for the American bishops, my research attempted to determine how priests regarded and lived this condition of celibacy (*The American Priest: Psychological Investigations,* Eugene Kennedy and Victor Heckler, USCC 1971).

We learned that even the healthiest priests in the sample did not perceive celibacy as a virtue to be practiced as much as a condition of life to which they had to adjust. This required an enormous investment of energy and often led them to do things—such as taking expensive vacations, having big cars, or costly hobbies—for which they were criticized. Other less healthy priests in the sample accepted celibacy for reasons varied and emotionally self-serving enough to raise questions about how sturdy a foundation it is for ministry.

An unexpected adjustment

Even then, many immature candidates found no challenge in celibacy because their own sexuality had not yet awakened within them and had not yet been integrated into their personality development. Because they were not attracted to marriage, celibacy was never a true existential choice for them. Often, their sexual feelings only asserted themselves after they had entered parish work. They were dismayed and puzzled by erotic attractions to boys that reflected their own pre-adolescent state. Celibacy for these men was an illusion of virtue, a stage set for life rather than a condition for service, and they found themselves abusing the trust that this presumed virtue won for them by seducing and defiling the innocent in their care. Their lack of maturity was reflected in their low-level denial and distorted descriptions of their behavior.

The more disturbed the priest, the more disturbed was the sexual adjustment he forged under the cover a celibate priesthood provided. It became apparent that celibacy existed far more for the purposes of the institution than the growth of seminarians or the good of the people. Celibacy sealed an all-male clergy totally dependent on the institutional church for identity and livelihood. While we all admire men and women who voluntarily choose, with full understanding of themselves and the sacrifice they make, to lead celibate lives, we must not look away from the high price this requirement exacts from the large majority of even healthy persons.

While celibacy obviously does not cause pedophilia, it provides a setting and a shield for candidates whose lack of inner maturity dilutes celibacy as both a challenge and a choice. It may, in some circumstances, incubate men who will lead tragic double lives behind its screen. All too often, it has provided an *as if* life of virtue for men deeply entangled in and tortured by sexual conflicts. When they act out these conflicts, they cause others misery whose measure we are just beginning to take.

The possibilities of celibacy as a freely chosen state of service are overshadowed by the documented realities of celibacy as a forced condition of becoming a clergyman in service to an institution. It is late in the day for popes to do what they have refused to do, despite the obvious evidence of celibacy as a problematic state: examine celibacy in depth for the sake of both their priests and their people.

5

The Celibacy Requirement for Priests Does Not Contribute to Child Sexual Abuse

Philip Jenkins

Philip Jenkins is a professor of history and religious studies at Pennsylvania State University and the author of Pedophiles and Priests.

Clerical celibacy does not, as many claim, reflect a hatred of women and contempt for sexuality. Indeed, people are misinformed about the nature and history of priestly celibacy. For example, celibacy did not develop during the Middle Ages as many think. In fact, priestly celibacy is a product of the early church, which believed that celibate priests would focus more on spiritual rather than worldly interests. Demanding that priests forgo sex in order to give themselves more fully to the church illustrates a respect for the power of sexuality, not contempt for it. Moreover, no evidence shows that abandoning celibacy would prevent child sexual abuse or reduce the numbers of homosexuals in the priesthood. Pedophilia and gay subcultures exist in churches where clergy are allowed to marry.

In March 2002, as cases of sexual abuse by Catholic clergy have appeared regularly in the headlines, the notion of priestly celibacy has become the subject of talk radio and dinner party discussions. But much of the debate has been rooted in myth and misinformation and clouded by the assumption, particularly in this country, that the time has come for the Roman Catholic Church to end this Medieval foolishness and do away with the practice. In fact, the subject is much more complex. And barring unforeseen circumstances, celibacy is likely to be around in the American Catholic church for a long time to come.

The popular view seems to be that celibacy reflects a hatred and con-

Philip Jenkins, "Celibacy for Beginners," *Washington Post*, March 31, 2002. Copyright © 2002 by Washington Post Book World Service/Washington Post Writers Group. Reproduced by permission of the author.

tempt for sexuality—and for women—and that it turns priests into frustrated loners who express their inner conflicts through sexual assaults on little children. For many reasons, I think these charges are unfair.

The history of celibacy

I belong to a church that does not require celibacy of its clergy and has female priests, namely the Episcopal Church. Yet speaking as a historian, I can understand the reasons another church might require priestly celibacy. And as a consumer of news, I see that celibacy's origins and the church's motivations in requiring it are widely misunderstood.

Let's start with what has become a standard misstatement about its genesis: That priests were required to be celibate beginning around 1100, maybe even a little later. We do know that compulsory celibacy was not a practice of the earliest church. We know that Saint Peter had a mother-in-law, that the apostles traveled in the company of their wives, and that some early popes were (without causing scandal) the sons of other popes. Yet beyond these facts, much is in doubt.

The notion that mandatory celibacy wasn't imposed until the 12th century, stated as "fact," seems quite damning to the church's insistence on the practice. If true, modern Catholics would be insisting on an innovation that has been around for less than half of the history of Christianity, one that dates to the Middle Ages, a period that enjoys a dreadful reputation in modern thought. Through guilt by association, celibacy seems to be linked in many people's minds with such horrors as witch-burning, the Inquisition and the Crusades. Worst of all, the reasons often cited for the invention of celibacy are not even spiritual, but rather involve land rights. According to a scholarly myth widely held among historians, the church was just trying to ensure that the children of priests could not become legitimate heirs to church land. Literally, according to this story, the modern Catholic Church is keeping alive a survival of feudal times.

Celibacy's origins and the church's motivations in requiring it are widely misunderstood.

This pseudo-history is wrong at almost every point. Mandatory celibacy goes much further back than Medieval times, if not quite to the days of the apostles. Priestly celibacy was the usual expectation in the West by late Roman times, say the 4th century, and Medieval statements on the subject were just reasserting discipline that had collapsed temporarily in times of war and social chaos. Of course we can find married priests throughout the Middle Ages, just as we can find priests committing molestation today, but that does not mean that, in either case, they were acting with church approval.

In making this point about dates, I am not just nitpicking in the worst academic tradition. I am stressing that priestly celibacy is a product of the very early church. Just how early? It was celibate priests and monks who made the final decisions about which books were going to make up the New

Testament, and which would be excluded. If, as most Christians believe, the ideas and practices of the early church carry special authority, then we should certainly rank priestly celibacy among these ancient traditions.

The reasoning behind celibacy

So if they were not defending land rights, why did successive popes try to enforce celibacy? Odd as this may seem, the main reason seems to have been the increased frequency of the Eucharist or Mass. Because of the need to focus on spiritual rather than worldly interests, married priests in the 3rd and 4th centuries were supposed to abstain from sex the night before saying Mass. As Mass became a daily ritual, this effectively demanded permanent celibacy. Out of this practical need came a whole theology of self-sacrifice. The idea of celibacy is based less on a fear of sexuality than on a deep respect for its power, and with proper training, a celibate could transform or channel this power into a source of strength. Modern psychologists would later invent the term "sublimation" for this complex process.

By giving up the most basic human needs and comforts, the priest was able to devote himself entirely to God and to the people he served. He was meant to treat all the faithful equally, with no need to give special preference to a wife or children. A "father" was meant to be father to all. Of course, changes in society mean that the church no longer needs to prove that its clergy stand above the narrow ties of kin, but other reasons for celibacy remain unchanged. In some ways, the case for celibacy may even be greater today than it was centuries ago. In a society that seems to be so thoroughly aware of sex and sexuality, maybe even obsessed with it, what greater self-sacrifice could there be, what greater rejection of the culture, than the adoption of celibacy?

At the same time, not even the Catholic Church claims that clerical celibacy is a strict matter of faith that can never be changed. The church indeed says that some of its teachings can never be softened—for instance, the prohibition on female priests or the ban on abortion. But it also makes clear that celibacy (like matters of liturgical practice, for example) is a question of internal church discipline, which could be changed if circumstances demanded it. Such a change would not require any embarrassing backtracking on past policies, any kind of reversal of once "infallible" statements.

It may come as a surprise that Catholic authorities do allow a little flexibility in the matter of married priests. If, for instance, a priest converts to Catholicism from a church that allows marriage, like the Orthodox, then he may be able to enter the Roman church as a married priest in good standing. Some have done so—often to the annoyance of mainstream Catholic clergy, who are not granted this same privilege.

Should the church change its stand?

But now let me ask an outrageous question: Why *should* the Roman Catholic Church change its stance on celibacy? Much has been said of late about the damage that celibacy inflicts on the modern church and its poor exploited believers. But, like the pseudo-history, many of these contemporary charges are false.

Among the harms caused by celibacy, two possibilities come to mind. One, obviously, is the problem of "pedophile priests," who allegedly commit their crimes because of the frustration and immaturity caused directly by celibacy. The reform motto is beautiful in its simplicity, and inspiring in its urgency: End celibacy and save the children! Yet there is no credible evidence to link the two. Many of the same problems also happen in churches and denominations that allow clergy to marry. Based on some excellent studies using large samples of priests, we can say that about 2 or 3 percent of Catholic priests are sexually involved with minors. There is no evidence that the rate for these priests is higher than that for any other non-celibate group. So how does celibacy come into the picture at all?

Another issue more plausibly connected with celibacy is the growth of gay subcultures in the American priesthood—not that having homosexual priests is necessarily bad in itself. But when men with gay inclinations are represented in the priesthood at a rate 10 or 20 times that in the average male population (which studies suggest is the case), this does tend to make the priesthood more of a closed caste separated from the lives of ordinary believers. But ending celibacy now almost certainly would not change the situation, or make the priesthood less gay. Just look at my own Episcopal church, in which clergy have been allowed to marry since the 16th century: The Episcopal clergy has flourishing gay subcultures quite as active as those rumored in the Roman church, only far more public.

Ultimately, the Catholic stance on priestly celibacy can change in one of two ways, neither of which seems very likely. The American church could go into schism, declaring its independence from Rome, which nobody is predicting. The only alternative is to wait for Rome and the global church to declare changes from the center, an idea that reformers have prayed for over the years. As the hopeful joke goes, at the Third Vatican Council, the pope will bring his wife; at the Fourth Vatican Council, the pope will bring her husband. Yet today, the chances for that sort of reform seem bleak.

There are any number of reasons the Roman Catholic Church might want to end mandatory celibacy for its clergy. It might rethink the theology of the whole matter; it might carry out surveys showing that a married priesthood would simply do a better pastoral job of ministering to the faithful. Above all, it might decide that ending celibacy is simply the only way to restore the numbers of the priesthood, and that seems to me an excellent idea—though as I say, I write as an outsider. But whatever it does, let the church decide its course on celibacy for the right reasons. Let it act according to the logic of its own principles, and not in response to bogus history and convenient mythology.

6

Practices Within the Catholic Hierarchy Encourage Child Sexual Abuse

Christopher Hitchens

Christopher Hitchens is a columnist for Vanity Fair.

Prohibitions against the abuse of children are common across cultures, and under normal circumstances, someone who sheltered a pedophile would be condemned and prosecuted. However, those in the Catholic Church who allow priests to sexually abuse children remain in office and seem surprised at the public's outrage. Catholic practices, including celibacy, sexual repression, and the need to gain authority over children, lead to a church hierarchy that contributes to the sexual exploitation of children.

You often hear it said that religion, or religious belief, has the effect of making people behave better even if the metaphysical claims of faith are ill-founded or untrue. Bertrand Russell mounted a spirited attack on this opinion, on what were mainly empirical grounds, in his essay *Why I Am Not a Christian*. Actually, I rather like to see arguments in defense of faith mounted in a utilitarian manner in their turn, because this represents a huge if unadmitted concession to secular morality. However, the falsity or inconsistency even of such a weakened position needs to be exposed every now and again and—while Russell dealt chiefly with the past—there is no time like the present.

A common prohibition

During the notorious "Moors Murders" case in Britain in the late 1960s, when a series of children were tortured to death and then buried in a remote and hilly territory, the conservative novelist John Braine wrote a furious response to liberal relativism and its then-fashionable saying that in such cases "We are all guilty." He could not, he said, consent to any such proposition. Nor could he blame anything so amorphous as "society."

Christopher Hitchens, "Pedophilia's Double Standard," *Free Inquiry*, vol. 21, Summer 2002.

Rather than do what the accused had done, *he would prefer to have died.*

I dare say that any reader of *Free Inquiry* would affirm the same, whether they were parents, grandparents, or not. The prohibition against cruelty or violence to infants is quite ancient and very common to all cultures, so that we remember the exceptions—Sparta, for example—very well.[1] It's probably encoded in us in some way; it hardly needs the very memorable condemnation that it receives from Jesus of Nazareth, who is supposed to have said that, rather than perpetrate such a hideous offense, it would be better for the guilty to have a millstone put around their necks and to try and hide their shame in the depths of the sea.

An outrageous exception

Given that, the existence of a vast pedophile ring in the United States in the twenty-first century is something more than an affront to "family values." And the fact that this ring is operated by named and senior churchmen, who continue to hold high office and to officiate at Sunday ceremonies, is something more than an outrage. Alleged "cultists" in Waco, Texas, who were only *suspected* of maltreating children inside their compound, were immolated by a bombardment of federal fire [on April 19, 1993]. The admitted and confessed enablers and protectors of rapists and child abusers are invited, at the most, only to resign their high offices. And even this suggestion is something that they feel strong enough to repudiate—and with indignation at that.

The Roman Catholic Church . . . has been behaving as if, without the opportunity for sex with the underage, its whole ministry would collapse.

No doubt there are some secular institutions, such as prisons, where the incidence of sexual torture and rape is, so to speak, part of the system. But even these places take some care to protect the underage from predators. What continually strikes the reader of each successive case involving the churches is that the ghastly recurrence is truly systematic, if not indeed routine. I do not wish to seem sectarian, but I will risk the accusation. The Protestant churches and some prominent synagogues in Florida and New York appear to have been bad enough, in resorting at once to denial and to cover-up. The Roman Catholic Church, however, has been behaving as if, without the opportunity for sex with the underage, its whole ministry would collapse.

If I knowingly sheltered a torturer and abuser of children, or lied about my knowledge of him, or (aware of his record) pressed him upon my neighbors as a child-minder or babysitter, and if I stood to profit by these actions or inactions, I would expect more from the forces of law and order than a dirty look. So intense is our obsession with this crime, in-

---

1. In Sparta physically deformed children were abandoned to die of exposure. At seven, healthy males were taken from their mothers and raised in brutal military schools run by older boys and men who had suffered the same upbringing.

deed, that many innocent teachers and even Website surfers have had their careers and lives ruined by even the suggestion of it. But here are the men of god, calmly engaged in the racket and evidently irritated by the resulting fuss.

Church practices exploit children

It is quite obvious that, with recidivism at this level, one must look to the actual practices of the Catholic Church. The celibacy requirement, which is peculiar to Catholic Christians, is obviously a part of it. So is the renowned insistence of the Catholic Church on gaining authority over children, for doctrinal reasons, at the earliest possible age. The authority that is exerted, often by newly ordained and unstable young men, is a teaching entirely drenched in the obsession with all kinds of sex, and in the requirement to repress or prohibit a huge list of sexual behaviors. Moving along the continuum of priestly and episcopal hierarchy, one finds elderly but somehow useless men who may never have abused a child themselves, but cannot quite see why there is any outcry. I wager that they would not act like this if they had had the chance to be fathers or grandfathers themselves. Instead, they wager their supposedly immortal souls on the dogma that denies this opportunity to their subordinates, or which recruits from the maladjusted and inadequate.

To need love or sex only from the innocent, or to be able to express your needs only in that way, is obviously a terrible punishment in itself and can, in some circumstances, even call upon our pity (and our dearly bought secular and scientific knowledge about the possibility of care and help). But to become a hardened exploiter of children as part of your vocation, and to be defended by a coalition of stone-faced, ignorant patriarchs and hysterical virgins, is a privilege known only to the most devout. So who will now say that religion, for all its vast intellectual shortcomings, at least encourages the average Joe to be good (as the practical definition of morality used to run) while nobody is looking?

7

The Catholic Church's Response to Child Sexual Abuse Is Adequate

Stephen J. Rossetti

Stephen J. Rossetti is a psychologist and president of St. Luke Institute, a private Catholic psychiatric hospital serving clergy. He is also a consultant to the U.S. Conference of Catholic Bishops' ad hoc committee on child sexual abuse.

The Catholic Church has responded to allegations of child sexual abuse by priests in the best interest of children. However, the general public has a distorted and oversimplified understanding of the problem, which ultimately could put more children at risk. For example, contrary to public opinion, not all child molesters are pedophiles and therefore incurable. Most child molesters abuse postpubescent minors and can be treated. Knowing that many priests who have sexually molested teenagers can be successfully rehabilitated, the Catholic Church has correctly chosen to treat such men. Indeed, rather than defrock and loose child abusers into society unsupervised, where they may abuse again, church leaders have reassigned them to supervised positions. The church has also acted correctly in choosing not to report all allegations of abuse to authorities. In many cases, the church is bound to protect the victims' and priests' confidentiality, and often, the allegations are made long after the law can do anything about them because the statute of limitations has run out.

When complex situations are given simplistic understandings and simplistic solutions, people will inevitably be hurt. The phenomenon of child sexual abuse, in the priesthood and in society at large, is a complex issue that does not admit of simple understandings or simple solutions. It is important that we examine the issue in greater depth; otherwise the church and society will not only repeat past mistakes but also make new mistakes in response. Most important, without a more in-

Stephen J. Rossetti, "The Catholic Church and Child Sexual Abuse: Distortions, Complexities, and Resolutions," *America*, vol. 186, April 22, 2002, p. 8. Copyright © 2002 by America Press, Inc. Reproduced by permission.

formed understanding and a more reasoned response, children will be no safer and may, inadvertently, be placed at even greater risk.

Examining misconceptions

I would like to discuss five major oversimplifications and distortions regarding child sexual abuse that have been publicly raised in April 2002.

1. All child molesters are pedophiles and all pedophiles are incurable. They are dangerous men who abuse scores of minors. There is no hope for them.

As with all distortions, there is some truth to these statements. There are child molesters who are pedophiles, that is, they are sexually attracted to pre-pubescent minors, and some molest scores of minors. These high-profile, notorious abusers, who capture public attention, are usually resistant to psychological treatment. One does not speak of trying to change or "cure" their sexual attraction to minors. While some pedophiles can be helped to control their sexual desires, many cannot. Since these persons pose an ongoing threat to society, after serving an appropriate prison term, they ought to live in a kind of lifelong parole setting with absolutely no unsupervised contact with minors.

Fortunately, real pedophiles are the exception among adults who sexually abuse minors. Most abusers are not pedophiles. Most abuse post-pubescent minors and, all things being equal, are much more amenable to treatment. While both pedophiles and those who molest post-pubescent minors have committed a heinous crime, it would be an error to apply exactly the same remedy to them all. With treatment and supervision, many adults who molest adolescents can go on to live productive lives. But prudence would still dictate that these adults should be supervised whenever interacting with adolescents.

The possibility of treatment

John Geoghan, for example, a former priest of the Archdiocese of Boston, reportedly molested over 100 children. He went through several treatment regimens, apparently to no avail. He is now in prison and will remain there for many years. On the other hand, most perpetrators of child sexual abuse are members or friends of the victims' own families, such as fathers, stepfathers, uncles, cousins or neighbors. Would we treat a father who molests his daughter in exactly the same fashion as we would a pedophile like John Geoghan? Indeed, both should be subjected to the law and ought to pay for their crimes. But the ability to rehabilitate the incestuous father is much better than the habituated pedophile. We would be better served if the father could be eventually returned to society with appropriate safeguards.

Fred Berlin, M.D., an international expert on the treatment of child abusers, reported a relapse rate of only 2.9 percent over a five- to six-year period among 173 lay abusers who were treatment-compliant. Similarly, a church-run facility recently followed for one to five years after treatment 121 priests who sexually molested post-pubescent minors. Of those who finished an intensive treatment program and continued in follow-up care, only three relapsed—2.5 percent. While we grieve for those who were molested by these offenders who relapsed, treatment and supervision probably saved many other children from being molested.

While both pedophiles and those who molest postpubescent minors have committed a heinous crime, it would be an error to apply exactly the same remedy to them all.

It is often suggested in the public forum that offenders molest scores of victims and that there is an enormously high rate of relapse. But such high statistics are taken from clinical studies using forensic populations, which is a more disturbed and dysfunctional sample. If we are serious about protecting children, it is time for the public and the psychologists they quote to use more up-to-date and sophisticated clinical data. A father who molests his daughter and a compulsive pedophile are very different in their clinical profiles. To fashion a proper response that is likely to be effective, society needs to understand the complex differences and develop appropriate responses. In the end, child safety depends upon it. Moreover, it is important to note that most priests who sexually molest minors are clinically more like the abusive father than the compulsive pedophile. John Geoghan is the rare exception, thank God.

Questioning a celibate priesthood

2. Priests are more likely to be child molesters than others because they are celibate. Celibacy distorts one's sexuality, and a celibate priesthood attracts a larger proportion of men with sexual problems.

The first half of this simplification has been largely discredited in media stories. Researchers and clinicians have generally accepted the fact that celibacy does not cause child sexual abuse. In fact, the sexual difficulties and inner psychological problems that give rise to child sexual abuse are largely in place long before a person enters into the formation process for a celibate priesthood. In addition, most adults who sexually molest minors are, or will be, married.

The second half of the statement, "a celibate priesthood attracts a larger proportion of men with sexual problems," is currently being debated. Some have said that we seem to have so many child molesters in the priesthood because celibacy attracts people with sexual problems. Is that true?

It is a complex problem that demands a complex answer. Some people with sexual problems seek out a celibate lifestyle in an unconscious attempt to escape their own sexuality. I know this for a fact because I have counseled some who admit the same. Nonetheless, it is dangerous to summarize from the particular to the general.

Evaluating basic assumptions

By analogy, one might say that it is likely that there are some people who enter the police force because of their own distorted needs for power, authority and violence. But I suspect the mayor and police chief would have some strong words for anyone who tried to suggest that the police force in general is power-hungry, controlling and violent. It is a logical fallacy to generalize based on particular cases.

This brings to light the basic assumption that underlies these distortions—namely, that priests are more likely to be child abusers than others in society. Is that true? The short answer is: we do not know. There are simply no prevalence rates of perpetration of child sexual abuse either in society at large or in the priesthood. The reason for the lack of data is inherent in the crime. It is very difficult to gather a sample of adult males and ask them if they have ever sexually abused a minor. Even if they told the truth, gathering such data would present thorny ethical and legal considerations.

The best the church can do to estimate the prevalence rate of sexual abuse of minors by priests is to count the number of priests who have "substantial" allegations of child sexual abuse against them and compare this number with the total number of priests.

When the Archdiocese of Boston reportedly released the names of 80 priests who had sexually molested minors over the last 50 years, people asked, "How can there be so many priests who abuse children? There are only about 800 priests in the archdiocese, so this represents 10 percent of our entire presbyterate!" But the numbers were misleading. On March 15, 2002, the official publication of the archdiocese, *The Pilot,* said the number of substantial allegations was approximately 60, and it is important to note that this number represents the total number of accused priests over 50 years. The editorial estimated that there were probably about 3,000 priests who served in the archdiocese during these 50 years, so the ratio is about 2 percent.

It is not true that bishops are circumventing the reporting requirements about child sexual abuse.

Similarly, the Archdiocese of Philadelphia recently went over its records since 1950. There were 2,154 priests who served during this time frame, and there were "credible allegations" against 35. This is about 1.6 percent. Likewise, the Archdiocese of Chicago reviewed its records. In the past 40 years, out of 2,200 priests who served, about 40, or 1.8 percent, had received credible allegations of abuse.

While one case is one too many, especially when perpetrated by a man with a sacred trust—a Catholic priest—the suggestion that priests are more likely to be child abusers than other males has yet to be established. In fact, the early statistics challenge that assumption and actually imply that the number of priests who molest could be lower. It would be reasonable to believe that the number of adult males who molest minors in society is at least as large. One need only speak with the dedicated and overworked social workers who staff our child protective services around the country to know that the percentage of adult males who molest minors is not insignificant. I conducted a survey of 1,810 adults in the United States and Canada and found that over 19 percent of them had been the victims of sexual molestation by an adult before the age of 18. This suggests that there are many perpetrators of child sexual abuse in our society. While we are shocked, and rightly so, that there would be 60 priests in the Archdiocese of Boston who have molested minors, we should be equally shocked at just how common child sexual abuse is throughout our society.

Exploring the link to homosexuality

3. We have so many child abusers in the priesthood because a celibate priesthood attracts homosexuals.

No mainstream researcher would suggest that there is any link between homosexuality and true pedophilia, that is, sexual attraction of an adult to pre-pubescent minors. In addition, most adults in society who sexually molest minors are not homosexually oriented.

The rejoinder to this is the fact that most victims of priests are young males. But this, too, is easily open to misinterpretation. Most priests who molest minors were themselves molested as minors; their sexual abuse of minors is for many of them a kind of re-enactment of their own abuse and may have little to do with their sexual orientation. I have known some heterosexually oriented males who molested young males.

Nonetheless, a significant number of priests who sexually molest minors are involved with post-pubescent adolescent males, about 14 to 17 years of age. It appears to be true that many in this sub-population of priest child-molesters are homosexually oriented. But theirs is a particular kind of homosexuality, which one might call "regressed" or "stunted." These homosexual men are emotionally stuck in adolescence themselves, and so are at risk for being sexually active with teenage males. The issue is therefore not so much homosexuality but rather their stunted emotional development.

The problem is not that the church ordains homosexuals. Rather, it is that the church has ordained regressed or stunted homosexuals. The solution, then, is not to ban all homosexuals from ordained ministry, but rather to screen out regressed homosexuals before ordination. Preparation for ordination should directly assess the seminarian's ability and commitment to live a chaste, celibate life.

We are in a dangerous period that is intensely emotional. Everyone, inside and outside the church, wants to find simplistic solutions. "Getting rid of homosexuals" from the priesthood will not be as successful as some predict in ridding the church of child abusers and in the end may cause even more human damage.

The reporting requirements

4. The U.S. bishops continue to be secretive about child sex abuse cases and fail to follow the law and report these cases to legal authorities. They cannot be trusted.

Much of the real energy behind the current furor is anger directed at the Catholic bishops. People feel betrayed. But since 1992 I have witnessed bishops tackling scores of cases with great care and solicitude for victims and perpetrators. Yet they are currently being depicted as being grossly negligent. How can we understand this apparent contradiction?

It is true that in a minority of cases, victims have been asked to sign "gag orders." The diocese agrees to settle a civil suit; it pays out a certain sum of money, and it stipulates that the victim will not publicly reveal what happened. In retrospect, this can be recognized as a mistake. While one can understand a bishop's desire not to "scandalize" people and to protect the church's image, such actions promote distrust and allegations of secrecy.

Nevertheless, it is not true that bishops are circumventing the reporting requirements about child sexual abuse. Again, the reality is much more complicated. In most states, child-abuse reporting laws require that suspected incidents be reported only if the victim who comes forward is still a minor. I called one state's child protective services and asked if they would investigate a report if the victim was no longer a minor. The answer was no.

Time will show that the bishops' actions were both prudent and in the best interests of all in society, especially our children.

One might then suggest that the bishop report the allegation of abuse to the criminal authorities. There are two problems with this. First of all, the law does not require the bishop to report the allegation if the victim is no longer a minor and the bishop has a concurrent obligation to maintain pastoral confidentiality with those who confide in him, just as a secular counselor would. If the law does not give him "permission" to break confidentiality and report the abuse, then he is obligated to protect confidentiality. Second, even if he did report the allegation of abuse to the criminal authorities, the statute of limitations may well have expired, and there is little hope that the justice system would be of any assistance. Unfortunately, only a minority of cases of child sexual abuse are successfully adjudicated criminally.

Making an analogy with my second profession as a psychologist might be helpful. As a licensed psychologist, I am a mandated reporter of child sexual abuse. If I learn of a case of child sexual abuse, and I know an identified victim who is still a minor, I am obliged to report such cases to child protective services. But if I am counseling a 40-year-old woman, for example, who reveals to me that her uncle abused her 25 years ago, should I report her uncle? In many states, the law does not require this. Most likely the woman would not want it reported. And in a therapeutic setting, I have an ethical and legal obligation to protect this woman's confidentiality and privacy. So since the law does not stipulate that I must break confidentiality to report the abuse, I am obligated by law to maintain her privacy.

A double standard

The bishops are being excoriated for not reporting cases of abuse. But the laws do not require it in most situations that the church faces. The bishops also have a pastoral obligation to maintain confidentiality. What many dioceses are doing is counseling the victims that they themselves are free to report the incident to civil authorities. In fact, the church should encourage victims to report such an incident. But one can clearly argue that unless the law requires the church to break confidentiality—which the law usually does not do—it is up to the victim to report.

A disturbing trend is now appearing. Legal authorities are demanding from Catholic dioceses a complete list of all past allegations against priests of child sexual abuse. In most cases, these legal authorities are going beyond the requirements of the law. They are setting up a kind of double standard that I believe should be tested in the courts. While church authorities may willingly comply, it is a dangerous precedent to have one standard for priests and another for the rest of society.

What is needed for the protection of children is not a different standard of reporting only for priests, but a better reporting system that sets a better standard for all; this ought to include revisiting the length of the statute of limitations in child sexual abuse cases.

5. The safest thing for children is to defrock any priest who is guilty of child sexual abuse. The church has been grossly negligent by continuing to shuffle such priests from parish to parish, where they re-offend.

It is true that the Archdiocese of Boston made a grievous error in reassigning John Geoghan to a parish after he became known as a child molester. There was no excuse for such an action. Any priest who sexually molests a minor should never be returned to parish ministry or any ministry involving minors. But I would say clearly that there have been very few cases of such actions since 1992. Even in Boston, almost all the priests with substantial allegations of child sexual abuse were either retired early, dismissed from ministry or placed in assignments not involving minors. Even in Boston, the case of John Geoghan is an exception, but it is being portrayed as if it were normal in the church.

This raises a more difficult question: should any priest who has a past history of molesting a minor remain in the priesthood? Clearly, the public is saying no. And I think public pressure will have its way. Around the country, priests with a substantial allegation of child molestation are being dismissed from any form of ministry. The damage to the church's credibility is so large, and the legal and financial fallout is so great, that many of our leaders feel forced to expel them all. This is certainly the safest action for the church.

The risk of zero tolerance

But is this the safest course of action for children? When priests are dismissed from ministry, they go out into society unsupervised and perhaps even untreated. Then they are free to do as they please. If they have been convicted of a sexual crime against minors, they may have to be registered in compliance with various state or local laws. But, as noted previously, there are few criminal convictions against child sex abusers. Either the statute of limitations has run out, or the victim does not want a criminal trial, or there is simply insufficient evidence. Whatever the reason, when the church "defrocks" these priests, they are no longer supervised. One might recall the case of James Porter, who was expelled from the Diocese of Fall River in Massachusetts and returned to life as a layman. He married and was eventually convicted of molesting his children's baby sitter.

The question of what to do with child molesters is complex. Some bishops have been sending priests accused of child sexual abuse for intensive psychotherapeutic treatment and then, depending upon the man's response to treatment, taking the ones who present the least risk and returning them to a limited, supervised ministry that did not involve direct contact with minors. Of the scores of such cases, very, very few have re-offended. The public has been outraged that these men were still in ministry at all. But I believe that time will show that the bishops' actions were both prudent and in the best interests of all in society, especially our children. If all these priests had been summarily dismissed from the priesthood, it is very probable that more children would have been abused. Putting a priest through treatment and leaving him in a limited ministry, such as that of chaplain to a convent or nursing home, is not without some risk. But there is more risk in releasing him into society.

The church must stand fast with its teachings and endure the wrath that will come in its wake.

In general, the bishops of the United States have done well in dealing with most cases of child sexual abuse by priests since 1992. There have been exceptions, and mistakes have been made. But there will always be mistakes made with such complex and difficult cases. On the surface, the matter seems easy. The public says, "The priest is charged with sexual abuse, so throw him out of the priesthood." But if the civil and criminal authorities will not prosecute the case—and in most cases they will not—who decides if the accused is guilty? Unfortunately and unfairly, this falls to the bishops. They have tried to do what is right and best for everyone. But public pressure is forcing them to dismiss them all. The bishops are acquiescing, and now these men become society's problem, not just the church's. I hope that society handles these cases well.

Underlying issues and needed resolutions

As the public furor continues and the intensity of the story continues, it is becoming clear that the presenting issues, named above, are only the tip of the iceberg. The ferocity and duration of the public response suggests that there are other underlying issues that are driving the intensity of the public's response. These underlying issues are harder to ascertain, but some are beginning to surface. I believe that we, as a church, need to determine what these issues are and discern what changes they are calling us to make. I have identified five underlying reasons; I have no doubt that there are more.

One of the underlying reasons, I believe, for the ferocity of the public's response is the emotional response of a parent to child sexual abuse. Parents have a strong, visceral response. There is a kind of healthy "parental rage" when their children are threatened or harmed. At times, when some in the church have not mirrored this rage, it is naturally said that they "don't get it." Our first resolution as church should be to listen to parents. We need to have parents on our diocesan pastoral councils, and these must have a real voice in diocesan leadership; parents need to be on our diocesan child-abuse review boards, and these review boards need to have a significant impact in the decisions of the diocese in abuse cases; and parents need to have the ear of the bishop just as much as do canon lawyers and priests.

A second issue coming through loud and clear is that society does not trust the way the bishops conduct their inner processes. While the bishops have generally dealt responsibly with child sex abuse cases, the public does not know what they have done. It is a general law of human nature that we do not trust what we do not know. Clearly, the current crisis signals the need for greater openness on the part of church leadership in this country. We not only need to deal with cases well, but the very processes we use need to be open to public scrutiny. We cannot presume the trust of the people. This second resolution must be to increase the openness of church leadership to public scrutiny.

Similarly, church leadership ought to couple this increased openness with public accountability. Church leaders must make clear their willingness to cooperate with legal authorities and government agencies. This accountability extends as well to all the people of God. The perception that they have not been responsive to these groups has resulted in their paying a heavy toll in eroding public trust. A third resolution must be to increase communication with and accountability to civil authorities and to the people of God.

Another resolution pertains to a more "spiritual" issue. The public expects church leaders to be who we profess to be. That is, they expect us to be people of integrity. We profess to be celibate priests and Christians. When we are neither, the public is scandalized. In recent days, our church has appeared to be neither humble nor chaste. The media will continue to "flog" us until we are duly humbled and chastened. It is a bitter lesson for us to learn. Our fourth resolution therefore must be one of integrity; we must strive to be the humble and chaste Christians that we profess to be. When we fail, we ought to expect a public chastening.

Preaching the truth

Finally, I add one last suggested resolution. The Catholic Church has some clear and controversial teachings in areas of human sexuality, such as sexual chastity, birth control, abortion, marriage and homosexuality. Modern Americans, Catholics included, disagree with many of these teachings. The profound disagreement gives rise to considerable distrust, hurt and bitterness. I suspect some of the current furor is a gushing forth of much of this pent-up anger. Nevertheless, the church must stand fast with its teachings and endure the wrath that will come in its wake.

The Gospel of Christ will not always be popular, nor can public opinion determine what we teach. Jesus promised his disciples that they would suffer for his teaching. If we are too well thought of by secular society, one might wonder how faithful we are to the challenging Gospel that Jesus gave us. One of my concerns in the current crisis is that the Catholic bishops of this country will be less willing or able to exercise their responsibilities as teachers. It is a duty they cannot shirk, no matter how they are perceived. The final resolution I offer the church is to continue to preach the truth.

People naturally do not like complexity and uncertainty, especially with upsetting realities like the sexual abuse of children. It may be that the public is currently being fed on simplistic understandings and simplistic solutions because we have great difficulty facing deeper truths. We want child sexual abuse to be the exclusive crime of a few perpetrators who are "out there" and not part of our families. We would like to accuse an identifiable group of deviants who are different from us. We want our lives and the lives of our children to be completely and absolutely free of risk. We want a clear and simple solution, but there is none. Facing the fact that the sexual abuse of children is a crime that not only occurs in the priesthood, but most of the time is perpetrated in our own families, is a most painful truth. Not facing the complexities of child sexual abuse makes our children less safe, and pointing the finger at a few while missing the many ignores the cries of children in our own midst.

It is time for our church and our society, for priests and for families to work together in a new partnership to combat the grave evil that is the sexual abuse of children.

8

The Catholic Church's Response to Child Sexual Abuse Is Inadequate

Stephen J. Pope

Stephen J. Pope is associate professor of theology and chair of the department of theology at Boston College.

In letters addressing the child sexual abuse crisis in the Catholic Church, Cardinals Bernard Law and Edward Egan provide explanations and excuses, but they do not accept moral responsibility for their failure to protect the victims of abuse and never apologize for their mistakes. Both cardinals try to explain away their actions by claiming ignorance, but such ignorance is morally negligent. While the laity seeks personal accountability from church leaders, Law and Egan use words that distance themselves and the church from the scandal. Rather than assign blame, the church should examine why its structure leads to such muddled thinking about moral responsibility and permits sexual abuse to occur.

What does it mean to apologize, to express contrition, and to take responsibility for the sex-abuse crisis in the church? Cardinal Bernard Law and Cardinal Edward Egan, among others, have been intensely scrutinized by the media for their handling of the sexual abuse of minors by priests. Archbishops and bishops may feel that they have apologized for their mistakes, publicly repented their errors, and taken steps, like "zero tolerance" and mandatory reporting to police, to insure this abuse will never recur. But an apology can mean one of two things: to excuse by explaining or to ask for forgiveness. The current spate of statements by the hierarchy leaves many critics, lay and clerical, unsatisfied and uneasy. Have bishops and archbishops fully accepted the moral responsibility for what they have done—or failed to do? Consider the rhetoric and moral moves that some have made.

On January 28, 2002, Cardinal Law said, "As archbishop, it was and is my responsibility to ensure that our parishes be safe havens for our children. I acknowledge that, albeit unintentionally, I have failed in that responsibility." His letter to Boston priests on April 12, 2002, explains the Father Paul Shanley [sexual abuse] case in terms of "inadequate record keeping," and suggests that the real blame should go to "those who deal with clergy personnel" (that is, not him). Law refers several times to "our mistakes" in the plural but never in the first-person singular. Errors become a matter of degree: "we" were "too focused" on "individual components of each case" and should have been "more focused on the protection of children." In fact, there is no evidence that the cardinal tried to protect the children of Saint Julia's Church when he allowed Father John Geoghan, who had a history of sexual abuse, to be transferred there and then placed in charge of the parish youth group—all the while keeping the pastor ignorant. In retrospect, Law says he should not have put so much "emphasis" on secrecy since sometimes it "inhibits healing and places others at risk." The cardinal also lists conditions—"a desire to protect the privacy of the victim, to avoid scandal to the faithful, and to preserve the reputation of the priest"—that are all legitimate values in the abstract, but they are used here as evidence of his own moral innocence. What is missing is a clear, resounding, unambiguous admission of personal moral guilt that cries out for forgiveness.

Have bishops and archbishops fully accepted the moral responsibility for what they have done—or failed to do?

Law is not alone. Cardinal Egan, in a letter to New York Catholics read from pulpits on April 22, 2002, says that he is deeply sorry "if in hindsight we also discover that mistakes may have been made." He offers a conditional apology but no admission of actual wrongdoing, without which it is impossible to know what exactly the apology concerns: behavior or attitudes? consequences of policies or their improper execution? defective judgments or malice? He also speaks in the plural. He regrets errors of judgment that might have been made rather than repenting bad choices. His subsequent explanation of his letter is revealing: "I have said what I thought I needed to say to the people, and I hope it worked" (*New York Times,* April 25).

Another common phrase, "it seemed reasonable at the time" offers another excuse. It suggests that an error of judgment was made, based upon inappropriate assumptions (that pedophilia could be cured or that a sexually abusive priest could exert willpower to reform his ways) or flawed evidence (the report of a therapist that a patient has been healed). Providing an explanation of behavior in terms of understandable epistemological conditions or causes subtly strives to exculpate the agent.

Ignorance is no excuse

But not all forms of ignorance excuse. Some ignorance is culpable, that is, morally negligent, because the agent should have known better. To be clear: this means that the bishops who moved predatory priests to different parishes either knew that the priests in question would continue to exploit minors, and were indifferent to that possibility; or that they did not know that the priests would continue to be engaged in such horrendous activity. The former suggests a lack of care, the latter a lack of wisdom, and both suggest a lack of charity. How could anyone not know of the likelihood that priests guilty of serial sexual abuse are likely to do it again, especially when placed in circumstances that may induce this behavior?

What is missing [from Cardinal Bernard Law's letter] is a clear, resounding, unambiguous admission of personal moral guilt that cries out for forgiveness.

How can either of these scenarios be true of shepherds committed to caring for their flocks? Some history may help. The moral theology operative in the mid-twentieth century assumed that sexual sins from adultery to incest could be corrected by going to confession and reforming the will. This assumption was reinforced by the therapeutic claim that sexual "diseases" could be "cured" with appropriate treatment and psychological support. If alcoholics could be "recovered and recovering," so pedophiles could be "recovered and recovering." Perhaps this twelve-step approach has helped some people suffering from sexual addiction. But by the middle of the 1980s there was evidence that repeat offenders would repeat their crimes. By the late 1980s neither moral assumptions about confession and willpower nor therapeutic claims for a cure prevailed. Failure to acknowledge this reality, at least by the end of the decade, looks more like culpable ignorance and moral negligence than "doing the best we can."

The claim, "we did not react properly," is vague, suggesting that some reaction, though not sufficient, was provided. Stating the fault in a general way distances the decision maker from specific choices and moral acts. The actions are described in the negative, as an omission rather than a commission, and thus are cast as less damning than the active doing of evil deeds. But, as the church clearly teaches, sins of omission are as evil as those of commission.

Placing the institution before the victim

The American cardinals, in their letter to priests from Rome on April 24, 2002, "regret that episcopal oversight has not been able to preserve the church from this scandal." "Regret" is not even an apology. The cardinals' letter laments inadequate supervision and ignores the fact that patterns of abuse were known and allowed to continue—sometimes on the basis of a letter of recommendation to local institutional authorities by archdiocesan officials. It also distances the church from the scandal, as if the scandal were some kind of alien intruder rather than the consequence of choices made by individuals.

No doubt archbishops and bishops want children and young people to be safe and want abusive priests to serve people with respect and dignity. The problems reside not in the bishops' failing to have good intentions for laity and priests, but in diverting their direct concern and active solicitude from the victims—past and future—to the abusive priests. Acting in "good faith" does not entail only our own individual good and that of our friends and coworkers. Good will is oriented to the common good. Social context sets criteria for subjective self-assessment, and in this case episcopal authorities appear to have made judgments on the basis of the primacy of institutional values. Those who ignored, or at least downplayed, the needs of the laity did so in part as a result of a lifetime of socialization. They were rewarded for their loyalty with promotion and institutional power, which in turn seemed to reinforce moral myopia.

Looking for more than excuses

There are three key terms that run throughout discussions of the crisis of the American church: apology, forgiveness, and responsibility. Each term has several connotations, which contributes to the confusion. An apology can be offered for a mistake, an explanation given for an error, and responsibility assumed for the correction of mistakes. An apology can also be offered for moral guilt, forgiveness requested for an inexcusable act, and responsibility accepted in the form of personal accountability for serious moral negligence. More often than not, the most criticized members of the hierarchy have attempted to explain their mistakes, whereas the laity wants an honest confession of guilt and a genuine request for forgiveness for inexcusable choices.

These approaches to the triad of apology/forgiveness/responsibility are not mutually exclusive. An apology can include a mixture of explanation and confession, as long as the former is not used for self-absolution. Forgiveness can embrace elements of explaining as well as of pardoning—provided that some significant component of moral guilt is genuinely acknowledged. The duty to accept accountability for past guilt is not voided by an intensified sense of responsibility to prevent abuses in the future—in fact, the former ought to make more poignant a sense of the latter.

The challenge of the current situation is not simply assigning degrees of blame to individuals—a task that extends beyond the acts of bishops and criminal priests to encompass layers of complicity by many members of the clergy and laity as well. Individuals will have to come to terms with their own degrees of responsibility. What is important is that this terrible series of scandals leads us, as church, to think more carefully about how the ethos and structures of our institution have led to these disordered patterns of thought and action. Examining these does not wait upon the Vatican or depend on the leadership of cardinals.

9

Zero Tolerance of Child Sexual Abuse in the Catholic Church Is Unfair and Un-Catholic

Tom Beaudoin

Tom Beaudoin is a visiting assistant professor of theology and religious education at Boston College.

Zero tolerance is a phrase designed to appease public outrage and is in part based on a need for revenge, a morally unacceptable motivation that goes against Catholic teachings. In Catholic teachings not all sins have the same moral severity nor should all receive equal punishment. Although all sexual abuse of children is abhorrent, the severity of each case of abuse by priests is different and should be punished accordingly. Zero tolerance, however, fails to consider the circumstances of each case and punishes all accused priests equally. Moreover, although zero tolerance suggests that the church will instantly defrock any priests accused of abuse, in fact, under the policy, errant priests will simply be released from active ministry. In an effort to look good, the bishops have sacrificed real justice by imposing a zero-tolerance policy.

In June 2002, the American Catholic bishops were under enormous pressure in Dallas, Texas, [at the annual meeting of the U.S. Conference of Catholic Bishops,] to show that they heard the victims of sexual abuse. They are to be applauded for their openness to learning from victims, from Catholic thinkers, and from the deep disappointment of Catholics who are enraged about this Catholic Watergate.

Unfortunately, the bishops settled on a terribly regrettable policy. Zero tolerance was born of a need for image recuperation and from an authentic attempt to reply to popular outrage. But it is a deeply flawed and even un-Catholic policy.

Tom Beaudoin, "Bishops' Haste Produces Un-Catholic Policy," *National Catholic Reporter*, August 2, 2002. Copyright © 2002 by Tom Beaudoin. Reproduced by permission.

Zero tolerance is a weasel phrase. What does it really mean? What person of good will, after all, knowingly tolerates child abuse or pedophilia? Though it has the ring of absolute finality, the phrase is not ultimately meant to signal anything coherent. Instead, it is designed for public consumption, to portray bishops as tough on abusers. "Zero tolerance" is now the brand du jour for institutions caught in scandal, from corporations to sports teams to churches. The unreflective zeal with which the phrase is used is the clearest clue to its slippery denotation.

Zero tolerance is not "zero" after all. If by zero tolerance is meant no abusers in the priesthood, then those found guilty should be defrocked. But the bishops' policy allows convicted abusers to remain priests, though removed from active ministry. Everyday lay Catholics will still have to support these priests directly or indirectly for the remainder of their lives—which in some cases will be many decades—unless the bishops have a plan to establish a separate fund to support the livelihood of these priests. If a priest is still authentically a priest, he should be allowed to work toward returning to ministry. If he is not authentically a priest, he should be defrocked.

Zero tolerance contradicts the countercultural tradition of the U.S. bishops' social teachings. In their stands for peace and economic justice, the bishops have been willing to offend mainstream Americans, including Catholics, in the name of a calm, rational fidelity to human dignity. But the zero-tolerance policy is at least in part based on an attitude of revenge toward offenders, a furious desire on the part of many Catholics to see guilty priests humiliated. Revenge, though, is never a morally suitable motivation—as official Catholic teaching on the death penalty holds.

Zero tolerance was born of a need for image recuperation and from an authentic attempt to reply to popular outrage.

Zero tolerance is a blunt object of punishment. All abuse is an offense against human dignity, but just as the severity of sins differs in traditional Catholic teaching, and the severity of punishment in civil law varies according to many factors, not all abuses are the same. In our overheated atmosphere, this is difficult for many to admit. A priest who briefly exposed himself to a teenager has not committed the same act as a priest who raped a minor. The bishops' policy does not take sufficiently into account the specific circumstances of each case: the suffering of the victim(s), the rehabilitation of the priest, the context and nature of the offending or abusive actions.

Zero tolerance creates a class of priests who must live the rest of their lives in limbo. These priests, if they retire to monasteries, will then have to be supported by religious orders, whose quarters will now become permanent guesthouses for this new class of priests. What will be the psychological cost to priests, and the economic cost to the church, of this official banishment and ostracism?

With more time for deliberation, the bishops would likely have taken seriously these flaws in their policy. But they acted in haste.

Like Enron and Worldcom [companies who defrauded their stock-holders], my church's leaders hid their deficits for years, betraying the everyday faithful. In their rush to burnish their image in Dallas, the bish-ops chose not justice, but a slogan, with all the precision of a billy club.

With their policy, the bishops have presented abusers as a sacrificial lamb to angry Catholics. In so doing, the bishops perhaps hope to escape through a side door as American Catholics and the media revel fix our eyes on the glossy logo of zero tolerance. With this policy, the hard work of real accountability in the church has been traded for a bag of silver me-dia reviews.

10

The Church's Zero-Tolerance Policy Is Unfair to Victims

Ross Mackenzie

Ross Mackenzie is a syndicated columnist who writes on a variety of issues, including foreign affairs, culture, and family.

When the victims of child sexual abuse and the Catholic laity called for zero tolerance of pedophile priests, they rightly wanted a policy that mandated forced removal from the priesthood of every abusing priest. However, the zero-tolerance policy agreed to by the American bishops at their June 2002 meeting in Dallas, Texas, failed to meet these demands. Some priests will receive special dispensations: They will keep their title, remain on the payroll, and retire with dignity—dignity denied their victims. Although some might forgive the bishops for their failure to impose absolute zero tolerance, the victims of child sexual abuse will not likely do so.

On June 13, 2002, in Dallas, Texas, the nation's Roman Catholic leaders blinked.

An archbishop had put the opportunity well: "This is a defining moment for us, a moment for us to declare our resolve once and for all . . . to root out a cancer in our church."

The bishops did a lot, no question. They did major surgery. But was it radical enough?

Yes indeed, they voted 239-13 for a 3,500-word document, and the haggling has begun about what it really means—haggling that will go on endlessly.

According to the news columns, the document requires the reporting of all claims of sexual abuse of a minor to civil authorities, and it establishes a national review board and local advisory panels—good things all. It also strips offending priests of key duties, including interaction with children. But it does not mandate the removal of priests with a history of molesting (even raping) the young (mostly boys). Nor does it seem to raise the bar for the accountability of bishops high enough—if at all.

Less than zero tolerance

Going into the Dallas meeting, the cry was for zero tolerance for the sexual sins of Catholic priests against minor parishioners. Instead of zero tolerance, Catholics were given a policy of something less. Not the defrocking of offending priests, not removal from the payroll, but a shuffling to back rooms or to other dioceses. The document reads: "Diocesan policy will provide that for even a single act of sexual abuse of a minor—past, present or future—the offending priest or deacon will be permanently removed from ministry" for "a life of prayer and penance."

Instead of zero tolerence, Catholics were given a policy of something less.

No mandated laicization, or forced departure from the church. According to a report in *The Washington Post*, "Several bishops said today they expect that laicization will be the norm for future cases, but that some past offenders, who are now in their 60s, 70s or 80s, might be allowed to remain priests with no public duties, living out their lives with dignity in monasteries or retirement homes." And according to the outraged head of a Catholic victims' group, many priests kept on the payroll will keep their priestly identity by being called "Father," and "if you retain the title 'Father,' you still have one of the most important tools of the trade of a sexual predator in the church."

So:

Closeting. More special dispensations and exceptions. Zero tolerance watered down to something else—to tolerating in the shadows, and to retirement in "dignity" for the most undignified of behaviors, verily behaviors whereby violating priests denied their victims precisely the dignity accorded them.

Let us be clear. The cliché "only time will tell" applies here: Of course only time will tell how effective what the bishops did in Dallas will be in restoring public and parishioner confidence in the Catholic Church. But the extent of the horror in the nation's foremost institution for civilizational good must not be understated: an estimated 1,500 of the 46,000 priests ministering to 64 million Catholics—on the prowl for sex among the children in the flock.

Such vile acts are sins against Nature, right reason, and the laws of God and men. They irremediably wound their victims. They fracture the trust of the laity in the clergy. Yet church leaders, in an hour, apparently forgiving of promiscuity and predation, voted overwhelmingly to let pederasts and pedophiles stay on church payrolls to work discreetly or to retire with their heads held high.

Tolerance. Forgiveness—isn't that what Christianity today is all about?

Perhaps the church leaders finally could not go with zero tolerance because of the havoc it would wreak in the priestly ranks—already depleted, as are many Protestant ones.

Some parishes will forgive both the offending priests and the bishops. Others—feeling thus uncomforted by the blinking bishops, feeling the problem unsquarely met—will not.

But it's hard to see how the victims will. And it's hard to see how the broad Catholic laity will if it comes to view the Dallas decision the way a community might view a decision by the authorities to maintain a sex offender in their midst—even to keep him on the payroll albeit with modified duties—instead of riding him out of town on a rail.

11

Homosexuality in the Priesthood Fosters Child Sexual Abuse

Rod Dreher

Rod Dreher is a senior writer for the National Review, *a conservative journal of news and opinion.*

Although questioning homosexuality in the priesthood is unpopular and many Catholics want to ignore the problem, the church must face the fact that a growing network of gay clergy is damaging the fabric of the Catholic Church. As the number of homosexual priests has increased, so have incidents of clergy sexual abuse of teenage boys. Indeed, because most victims are teenagers, not children, the problem is clearly not pedophilia per se but homosexuality. Some authorities connect the increasing power and influence of homosexual priests with the abandonment of both the practice and the teaching of sexual morality, especially chastity. To solve the crisis of child sexual abuse in the Catholic Church, American bishops must explicitly discourage gay ordination, despite fears that reform will reduce already low numbers of priests entering the priesthood. In addition, church leaders must impose zero tolerance of errant sexual behavior and return to teaching Catholic sexual morality.

The first thing to understand about the Catholic Church's pedophilia scandal is that it is not technically a pedophilia scandal. Despite the gruesome example of defrocked Boston priest John Geoghan, whose case started the tidal wave of revelations, the overwhelming majority of priests who have molested minors are not pedophiles—that is, like Geoghan, among the rare adults sexually attracted to pre-pubescent children. They are, rather, "ephebophiles"—adults who are sexually attracted to post-pubescent youths, generally aged 12 to 17. And their victims have been almost exclusively boys.

Stephen Rubino, a New Jersey lawyer, says that of the over 300 al-

Rod Dreher, "The Gay Question: Amid the Catholic Church's Current Scandals, an Unignorable Issue," *National Review*, vol. 43, April 22, 2002, pp. 35–37. Copyright © 2002 by National Review, Inc. Reproduced by permission.

leged victims of priest sex abuse he has represented, roughly 85 percent are boys, and were teenagers when the abuse occurred. Dr. Richard Fitzgibbons, an eminent Catholic psychiatrist who has treated scores of victims and priest-perpetrators, says 90 percent of his patients were either teen male victims of priests, or priests who abused teen boys.

"I think we have to ask the question: Why are 90 percent to 95 percent, and some estimates say as high as 98 percent, of the victims of clergy [abuse] teenage boys? . . . We need to ask that question, and I think there's a certain reluctance to raise that issue," said the Reverend Donald B. Cozzens, author of *The Changing Face of the Priesthood,* on a recent *Meet the Press.*

The risk of raising questions

The reluctance arises, no doubt, partly out of a fear of antagonizing homosexual anti-defamation groups, who resent the stereotype of male homosexuals as pederasts. It's much safer to focus inquiry on the question of mandatory celibacy, or the issue of ordaining women. Yet it defies common sense to imagine that an ordinary man, having made a vow not to marry, is therefore going to be sexually attracted to boys. Indeed, suppose the Second Vatican Council in the 1960s had admitted married men to the ranks of the Catholic priesthood: Would a single adolescent boy molested over the past 40 years have escaped his fate? Similarly, if women had been ordained, would that somehow have made sexually predatory gay priests disappear?

No, this is chiefly a scandal about unchaste or criminal homosexuals in the Catholic priesthood, and about far too many in Church leadership disinclined to deal with the problem—or, worse, who may in some cases be actively involved in the misconduct. For Catholics, to start asking questions about homosexuality in the priesthood is to risk finding out more than many Church members prefer to know. For journalists, to confront the issue is to risk touching the electrified third rail of American popular culture: the dark side of homosexuality. Yet when we learn that the greatest crisis the Catholic Church in America has ever faced has been brought upon it almost wholly by male clerics seducing boys, attention must be paid to the man behind the curtain.

It is true that a great many gay people are sickened and appalled by what these wicked priests have done to boys, and some with a public voice, like journalist Andrew Sullivan, have vigorously denounced it. At the same time, Sullivan has strongly supported the ministry of gay priests.

A population of homosexual priests

How many gay priests are there? No one can say with certainty; the American bishops have never formally studied the issue, and, for obvious reasons, it is all but impossible to determine an accurate number. Richard Sipe, a laicized priest and psychotherapist who has studied the phenomenon of priests and sex abuse for most of his 40-year career, believes 20 percent of Catholic priests are homosexual, and that half of those are sexually active. In his book, Father Cozzens cites various studies putting the total much higher, but these surveys typically suffer from methodological problems that skew the numbers upward.

But those who lowball the numbers could equally be accused of wanting to downplay the problem. The Reverend C. John McCloskey, a member of the conservative Opus Dei organization, claimed recently that the number of gay priests is "two percent to four percent at a maximum," or equivalent to the estimated number of homosexuals in the general population; if that were true, however, it would be hard to explain why, according to experts, Catholic priests are dying of AIDS at a higher rate than males in the general population.

The "lavender Mafia"

The raw numbers are less important, though, if homosexual priests occupy positions of influence in the vast Catholic bureaucracy; and there seems little doubt that this is the case in the American Church. Lest this be dismissed as right-wing paranoia, it bears noting that psychotherapist Sipe is no conservative—indeed, he is disliked by many on the Catholic Right for his vigorous dissent from Church teaching on sexual morality—yet he is convinced that the sexual abuse of minors is facilitated by a secret, powerful network of gay priests. Sipe has a great deal of clinical and research experience in this field; he has reviewed thousands of case histories of sexually active priests and abuse victims. He is convinced of the existence of what the Reverend Andrew Greeley, the left-wing clerical gadfly, has called a "lavender Mafia."

> *For Catholics, to start asking questions about homosexuality in the priesthood is to risk finding out more than many Church members prefer to know.*

"This is a system. This is a whole community. You have many good people covering it up," Sipe says. "There is a network of power. A lot of seminary rectors and teachers are part of it, and they move to chancery-office positions, and on to bishoprics. It's part of the ladder of success. It breaks your heart to see the people who suffer because of this."

In his new book, *Goodbye! Good Men,* Michael S. Rose documents in shocking detail how pervasive militant homosexuality is in many seminaries, how much gay sex is taking place among seminarians and priest-professors, and how gay power cliques exclude and punish heterosexuals who oppose them. "It's not just a few guys in a few seminaries that have an ax to grind. It is a pattern," says Rose. "The protective network [of homosexual priests] begins in the seminaries."

The stories related in Rose's book will strike many as incredible, but they track closely with the stories that priests have told me about open gay sex and gay politicking in seminaries. The current scandal is opening Catholic eyes: As one ex-seminarian says, "People thought I was crazy when I told them what it was like there, so I finally quit talking about it. They're starting to see now that I wasn't."

Goodbye! Good Men links homosexuality among priests with theological dissent, a connection commonly made by conservative Catholics who wonder why their parish priests have practically abandoned teaching and explaining Catholic sexual morality. But one veteran vocations-team member for a conservative diocese cautions that Catholics should not assume that theological orthodoxy guarantees heterosexuality or chastity. "You find [active homosexuality] among some pretty conservative orders, and in places you'd not expect it," he says. "That's what makes this so depressing. You don't know where to turn."

An especially nasty aspect of this phenomenon is the vulnerability of sexually active gay priests and bishops to manipulation via blackmail. Priests, psychiatrists, and other informed parties say they encounter this constantly. "It's the secrecy," says Stephen Rubino. "If you're a bishop and you're having a relationship, and people know about it, are you compromised on dealing with sexually abusive priests? You bet you are. I've seen it happen."

Longtime observers predict that bishops and priests will be forced to resign under fire after their closeted homosexual lives, including sexual abuse, become public. The disgraced pederast former bishop of Palm Beach, Florida, J. Keith Symons, is probably not alone. If this happens, the Vatican will face mounting pressure from the Catholic rank-and-file to take action. As Father Greeley has written, "The laity, I suspect, would say it is one thing to accept a homosexual priest and quite another to accept a substantially homosexual clergy, many of whom are blatantly part of the gay subculture."

Examining church policy

Rome has explicitly discouraged the ordination of homosexuals since at least 1961. For the past decade, the Vatican has been ratcheting up the pressure against gay ordination—to little avail in most U.S. dioceses. In 2001, Archbishop Tarcisio Bertone, a top Vatican official, said gays should not be admitted to seminaries, a line that was reinforced in early March 2002 by the Pope's spokesman, Joaquin Navarro-Valls. Reports indicate that the Vatican may release another document to restate and clarify this policy.

Those who defend allowing homosexuals into the priesthood point to the Church's official teaching, which distinguishes between homosexual orientation (which the Church does not consider sinful) and homosexual acts (which the Catechism labels "grave depravity"). There is nothing wrong, the argument goes, with ordaining a homosexually oriented man committed to living chastely and to upholding the Church's teaching on sexuality. Surely there are many such faithful priests in service.

Rome has explicitly discouraged the ordination of homosexuals since at least 1961.

This argument, though, seems persuasive only under conditions far removed from those under which priests have to live. We have a culture in which there is little support for chastity, even from within the ranks of the Catholic priesthood. Conservative theologian Michael Novak says he is not prepared to argue for the exclusion of homosexuals from ordination, but as an ex-seminarian, he strongly believes gays should not be on seminary faculties, directing the formation in chastity of young men. Other Catholics who are more liberal than Novak on many Church issues go further on the question of gay ordination: Sipe believes gays shouldn't be admitted into seminaries at the present time—for their own protection, against sexual predators among the faculty and administration, who will attempt to draw them into a priestly subculture in which gay sex is normative behavior. Father Thomas P. Doyle, another critic of celibacy who has been deeply involved in the clergy-abuse issue, concurs: "Ordaining gay men at this time would be putting them, no matter how good and dedicated, in a precarious position."

Getting tough on gay ordination

No one wants to stigmatize homosexuals as abusers, because most of them are not. Still, it's hard to gainsay the contention that if there were few homosexuals in the priesthood, the number of sex-abuse victims today would be drastically lower. "We're learning a significant lesson from all this," says Dr. Fitzgibbons. "We have to protect our young. The protection of children and teenagers is more important than the feelings of homosexuals."

Though the American scandal is nowhere near played out, it seems likely that the barrage of humiliating revelations and mounting financial losses will force the Vatican to get tough on gay ordinations. To have any hope of being effective, Rome will have to clean house at most American seminaries. This can be done only if local bishops can be trusted to be both loyal to Rome and resolute—and that will happen only if the Vatican forces them to be accountable.

It's hard to gainsay the contention that if there were few homosexuals in the priesthood, the number of sex-abuse victims today would be drastically lower.

That still leaves the problem of current and future priests who are both homosexual and unchaste. It is true that most of the abuse cases that have reached the public's attention today involve older priests, and the situation in the seminaries has apparently been reined in somewhat from the anything-goes heyday of the 1970s and 1980s. Nevertheless, the problem is still enormous. Most of the cases reported in *Goodbye! Good Men* involving homosexual corruption date from recent years. One priest who left his seminary teaching post in the mid 1990s in despair over rampant homosexuality—and episcopal indifference to it—told me ominously: "The things I have seen in my years there are probably previews of coming attractions."

A return to the faith

The only sensible response, it would seem, is a zero-tolerance policy when it comes to sexual behavior by clergy, even between consenting adults (homosexual and heterosexual). The laity has a role to play as well. In a much-discussed essay in the November 2000 *Catholic World Report,* the Reverend Paul Shaughnessy, a Jesuit priest, suggested that lay Catholics seeking reform should help keep their priests accountable. He urged lay Catholics to use their checkbooks to fight sexual corruption, by steering their donations away from scandal-ridden dioceses and religious orders, and sending them instead to clean groups like Mother Teresa's Missionaries of Charity—and then letting the bishop or religious order know what they've done and why.

There is tremendous fear among churchmen that the kind of changes needed to put the Church aright will result in a severe loss of numbers in the priesthood at a time when vocations are already at a historic low. That is probably true in the short run, but the experience of a handful of American dioceses in which the local bishop is openly orthodox and willing to defend Church teaching without compromise gives reason to hope that a strong dose of traditional medicine can go a long way toward curing the Church's ills.

In 1995, Archbishop Elden Curtiss of Omaha published an article pointing out that dioceses that promote rigorous fidelity to Church teaching and practice produce significantly more vocations than do the moderate to liberal majority. Seminaries like Mount Saint Mary's in Emmitsburg, Maryland—where men know they will be supported in their authentic Catholic beliefs and practices, and in their commitment to celibacy and chastity—are filled to capacity.

This is not to suggest that the crisis gripping the Catholic Church in America can be entirely solved by a restoration of rigorously orthodox theology. Another problem that has to be addressed is the clericalist bias seriously afflicting the judgment of many bishops: Even Curtiss himself erred recently, by keeping an Omaha priest in ministry after the priest admitted having a child-pornography problem. But a return to the basics has to be a big part of a comprehensive solution. There is every reason to believe that a conservative reform—replacing dissenting or milquetoast bishops with solid, no-nonsense men; making the seminaries safe places for heterosexuals loyal to Church teaching; and restoring the priesthood to a corps of chaste, faith-filled disciples—would result in a tide of good men seeking holy orders.

This has already been happening in dioceses like Omaha; Lincoln, Nebraska; Denver; Peoria, Illinois; Fargo, North Dakota; and Arlington, Virginia. The road map that points the way to an authentic renewal of the Catholic priesthood is being drawn up in those places. And if you want to see the alternative—what would happen if the U.S. Church simply stayed on its current course—just read the morning papers.

12

Catholic Bishops Must Reform to Resolve the Child Sexual Abuse Crisis

Michael Sean Winters

Michael Sean Winters writes frequently on Catholic issues.

Bishops who protect pedophiles and who fail to accept responsibility for their failure to safeguard victims should not be allowed to lead in the Catholic Church. The philosophy of the Catholic hierarchy—to serve the local church, not to govern it—should be revived. Although strict reform regarding pedophile priests is important, to prevent future scandals and restore the credibility of the church, the bishops themselves must reform. Bishops who fail to accept responsibility for their failure to protect children should step down; bishops who acknowledge that they are human and accept responsibility for their failure to prevent child sexual abuse should remain to lead and to help reform the church.

At its June 2002 general meeting in Dallas, the Catholic bishops of the United States adopted a "one strike, you're out" policy that will remove from active ministry any priest who has sexually abused a minor, whether that abuse occurred 40 years ago or occurs tomorrow. It was a bold and important step, and it has brought the bishops considerable grief. Many in the press have slammed them for not going further and automatically "defrocking" abusive priests. But this is theological illiteracy posing as moral absolutism. It is a cornerstone of Catholic theology that the ordination of a man changes him ontologically—once a priest, always a priest. The ordination of a priest is a sacrament, and in a sacrament we believe God is the primary actor. God baptizes a child, ordains a man, marries a couple. Therefore defrocking is a complicated and cumbersome process, which never strips the priest absolutely of certain powers, like absolving sins or confecting the Eucharist. The policy adopted in Dallas upholds this theology while ensuring that by removing pedophile priests from active ministry—that is, from direct contact with the laity—no

Michael Sean Winters, "Service Station: Can Bishops Reform Themselves?" *New Republic*, vol. 227, July 1, 2002, pp. 14–16. Copyright © 2002 by The New Republic, Inc. Reproduced by permission.

priest gets a second chance to abuse a child. In fact, it may do more to protect children than defrocking would: Rather than letting an abuser loose in society, the bishops' new policy will keep him in a monastery repenting his sin and praying for the salvation of all.

The problem in Dallas was not the bishops' treatment of priests; it was their treatment of themselves. It is obvious to the average Catholic why a priest who is psychosexually ill can never be permitted to serve as a priest again. But by the same logic, why should the bishops who protected the pedophiles be permitted to continue in their offices? We can forgive Bernard Cardinal Law, as we can forgive John Geoghan; this was never a crisis about God's mercy. But just as we do not want John Geoghan near children, we are not sure we want Cardinal Law near power. The president of the conference, Bishop Wilton Gregory, pointed the way in his opening speech in Dallas: "We [bishops] are the ones who worried more about the possibility of scandal than in bringing about the kind of openness that helps prevent abuse. . . . We ask your forgiveness." With those words Bishop Gregory showed that finally someone in authority "gets it."

A return to the philosophy of service

But they are still only beginning. The bishops must rethink the manner in which they govern the Church. And that means they must radically revive the hierarchical philosophy on which Catholicism is based: that ministry and authority in the Church are always seen theologically as service. To govern the local church is to serve the local church. Every Holy Thursday, Catholics remind themselves of this when the priest or bishop washes the feet of twelve parishioners, recalling Jesus' washing the feet of the twelve apostles. In the Church's conception of hierarchy, authority goes up the ladder in consequence of the service and love coming down.

Ministry and authority in the Church are always seen theologically as service. To govern the local church is to serve the local church.

Too often, however, the theological idea of hierarchic service has been inverted. One hundred years ago the future Pope Pius X wrote: "When we speak of the Vicar of Christ [the Pope], we must not quibble, we must obey: we must not . . . evaluate his judgments, criticize his directions, lest we do injury. . . ." This is not obedience; it is slavishness. A lot has changed within the Catholic Church since 1902. The Mass is no longer in Latin; parishes have altar girls; the concept of separation of church and state is no longer condemned as a heresy. And it's true that in Dallas many of the bishops' decisions furthered a culture of openness: Pedophilia settlements will not be kept secret unless the victim requests it; a national review board will compile data from each diocese to verify compliance with the "one strike, you're out" policy; information about abuse will be turned over to civil authorities immediately. All these steps will help change the culture of the hierarchy. But not enough. Clearly some bishops believe they are accountable to no one but the Pope. And, under canon law, the Bishops' Conference has no juridical authority to police its own members beyond common shame, which evidently does not work. Nor do local synods function to chastise errant bishops. Throughout the nineteenth century the bishops and priests of a region played a central role in selecting new bishops, and there was a resulting sense of collegial responsibility; today Vatican-appointed diplomats propose the names from which the Pope selects new bishops.

Recommendations for reform

So what must the bishops do? For starters, they can listen to their laity, who are devoted to the Church but devoted also to change. Clearly in 2002 most Catholics in the United States love our Pope, even when we disagree with him. We are not following in the footsteps of the Synod of Pistoia, which in late-eighteenth-century Italy expressed its frustrations by refusing to acknowledge papal authority and insisting on appointing its own bishops. So rather than viewing their parishioners as potential schismatics corrupted by a Protestant societal ethos, the bishops should listen to American Catholicism's moderate voices for change—like Voice of the Faithful, a lay reform group that has emerged in Boston and elsewhere and has been advocating sensible changes in the Church. There is no theological reason why bishops must control the finances of a diocese or why lay people cannot play a greater role in selecting pastors and reviewing the bishops' decisions.

[The bishops] must preach about mercy from within the crisis, not as if it had not happened or as if the blame lay with others.

The bishops must also acknowledge that for some of their number, leadership is no longer an option. The depositions in Boston continue: Whatever good Cardinal Law has done in the past—and Law has done great good in the past—his legacy now is the sight of his protégés entering courtrooms. In New York, Cardinal Edward Egan may have escaped criminal charges for allegedly failing, as bishop of Bridgeport, Connecticut, to meet the state's mandatory reporting requirements on sexual abuse of minors; but the moral stain perdures. Sooner or later, gracefully or pitifully, both men must go. On the other hand, Bishop Gregory has emerged as a man of moral clarity and decisive leadership. Give that man a red hat.

Lastly, the bishops must literally preach their way out of this crisis. They must preach about mercy from within the crisis, not as if it had not happened or as if the blame lay with others. They must demonstrate why we should again consider them spiritual guides and leaders. Compare Bishop Gregory's forthright apology quoted above to that of Cardinal Egan's "apology" in April 2002: "If in hindsight we also discover that mistakes may have been made as regards prompt removal of priests and assistance to victims, I am deeply sorry." Which man had recently consulted his lawyer, and which man had recently consulted his Bible?

The prodigal bishops?

In that Bible, one finds the parable of the prodigal son. It is a most diffi-cult parable for many preachers, and I remember the awkwardness my Sunday school teacher had in explaining it to me when I was eleven years old. It seems unfair: We are told to be good, and we strive to be good, and then the slacker turns around and gets the fatted calf and the fancy coat. We do not want to believe that God's mercy counts for more than our ef-forts to be good. The parable is especially offensive if one is a 70-year-old bishop who has climbed his way to an office of prominence and author-ity through hard work and sacrifice. But this is precisely what Christians are called to believe. It is why pride, not lust, is the deadliest of the seven deadly sins. It is why the Church needs leaders who are not "holier than thou" but who are as human as the rest of us. It is why, if the bishops reach deep, this moment could become a great moment in the history of Catholicism, a time when we again learn to preach the outrageous propo-sition that God's mercy outruns God's justice.

"A man had two sons. . . ." There are no four words that have greater resonance in a Christian's soul than these, and none is more needed by the Catholic Church in the United States at this moment. We Catholics love our bishops; or, better to say, we want to love them again. In declining to resign, Cardinal Law said that as a bishop he is the father of the family and that a father does not abandon the family when times get tough. He mis-understands. Today Cardinal Law and his brother bishops are in the place of the prodigal son. But, of course, the prodigal turned around. [Law re-signed in December 2002.]

13

Child Sexual Abuse in the Catholic Church Should Be Treated as a Crime

Thomas Szasz

Thomas Szasz is a professor of psychiatry emeritus at the State University of New York, Upstate Medical University in Syracuse, New York. Szasz is a controversial figure in psychiatry since the publication of his book The Myth of Mental Illness.

Priests who have sexually abused children and the cardinals who fail to turn these priests over to the authorities try to escape responsibility for these reprehensible acts by defining child sexual abuse as a disease rather than a crime. Unfortunately, those who classify child sexual abuse as a disease have confused disease with immorality. Claiming that pedophile priests simply suffer from a disease suggests that their actions have consequences to them alone and are therefore not punishable. Such a view holds that pedophilia, as a disease, should be treated. However, adults who have sex with children are harming them and should be punished. Priests who choose to act on their sexual desires and molest children do not have a sexual disease that can be treated away; they are committing an act that society has determined is both immoral and criminal.

We use words to label and help us comprehend the world around us. At the same time, many of the words we use are like distorting lenses: They make us misperceive and hence misjudge the object we look at. As Sir James Fitzjames Stephen, the great 19th-century English jurist, aptly put it, "Men have an all but incurable propensity to prejudge all the great questions which interest them by stamping their prejudices upon their language."

Consider the ongoing scandal involving Roman Catholic priests accused of molesting boys. American law defines sexual congress between an adult and a child as a crime. The American Psychiatric Association defines it as a disease called "pedophilia."

Thomas Szasz, "Sins of the Fathers: Is Child Molestation a Sickness or a Crime?" *Reason*, vol. 34, August 2002, pp. 54–60. Copyright © 2002 by Reason Foundation. Reproduced by permission.

Mixing concepts

Crimes are acts we commit. Diseases are biological processes that happen to our bodies. Mixing these two concepts by defining behaviors we disapprove of as diseases is a bottomless source of confusion and corruption.

That confusion was illustrated by a February 8, 2002, letter to *The Boston Globe* in which the Reverend John F. Burns defended Boston Cardinal Bernard Law against critics who said he ought to resign. As an archbishop, Law had transferred the Reverend John J. Geoghan to a new parish despite allegations of sexual abuse. Geoghan eventually was accused of molesting more than 100 children over three decades.

"It should be noted that neither Cardinal Bernard Law nor Father John Geoghan was aware early on of the etiology or pathology of the disease of pedophilia," Burns wrote. "The cardinal did what an archbishop does best. He showed kindness and love to an apparent errant priest. Father Geoghan also did what more recent knowledge shows pedophiles do: namely, be in total denial, with hardly any remembrance or remorse for their diseased acts. Calling for the cardinal's resignation is absurd. Let the healing begin and the law take its course."

The uncertainty introduced by viewing sexual abuse as the symptom of a disease played an important role in the church's failure to protect congregants from [pedophile] priests like [John] Geoghan.

The law is taking its course not only in the suits filed against the church by the victims of Geoghan and other abusive priests. Geoghan himself has been convicted of molestation in one case and faces trial in another. But if his behavior was caused by "the disease of pedophilia," a condition that not only compelled him to fondle boys but erased his memory of those "diseased acts," how can it be just to punish him? The uncertainty introduced by viewing sexual abuse as the symptom of a disease played an important role in the church's failure to protect congregants from priests like Geoghan. In a May 8, 2002, deposition, Cardinal Law was asked how he approached molestation charges. "I viewed this as a pathology, as a psychological pathology, as an illness," he said. "Obviously, I viewed it as something that had a moral component. It was, objectively speaking, a gravely sinful act." The combination of these two irreconcilable views, medical and moral, was a recipe for inaction.

The medical penal establishment

Today virtually any unwanted behavior, from shopaholism and kleptomania to sexaholism and pedophilia, may be defined as a disease whose diagnosis and treatment belong in the province of the medical system. Disease-making thus has become similar to lawmaking. Politicians, responsive to tradition and popular opinion, can define any act, from teaching slaves to read to the cold-blooded murder of a bank guard, as a crime whose control belongs in the province of the criminal justice system.

Applied to behavior, especially sexual behavior, the disease label combines a description with a covert value judgment. Masturbation, homosexuality, and the use of nongenital body parts (especially the mouth and anus) for sexual gratification have, at one time or place, all been considered sins, crimes, diseases, normal behaviors, and even therapeutic measures. For many years psychiatrists imprisoned homosexuals and tried to "cure" them; now they self-righteously proclaim that homosexuality is normal and diagnose people who oppose that view as "homophobic." Psychiatrists diagnose the person who eats too much as suffering from "bulimia" and the person who eats too little as suffering from "anorexia nervosa." Similarly, the person who has too much sex suffers from "sex addiction," while the person who shows too little interest in sex suffers from "sexual aversion disorder." Yet psychiatrists do not consider celibacy a form of mental illness; celibate persons are not said to suffer from "anerotica nervosa."

Why not? Because psychiatrists, politicians, and the media respect the Roman Catholic Church's definition of celibacy as a virtue, a "gift from God," even though celibacy is at least as "abnormal" as homosexuality, which the church continues to define as a grievous sin—an "intrinsic evil," in the words of Cardinal Anthony Bevilacqua. Regardless of how unnatural or socially destructive a pattern of sexual behavior might be, if the church declares it to be virtuous—as with celibacy or abstinence from nonprocreative sexual acts—psychiatrists do not classify it as a disease. Thus a religion's moral teachings shape what is ostensibly a scientific judgment.

Confusing disease with moral judgment

Conversely, psychiatric diagnoses affect moral judgments. Fred Berlin, founder of the Johns Hopkins Sexual Disorders Clinic and a professor of psychiatry at the Johns Hopkins School of Medicine, declares: "Some research suggests that some genetic and hormonal abnormalities may play a role [in pedophilia]. . . . We now recognize that it's not just a moral issue, and that nobody chooses to be sexually attracted to young people." Yet an action that affects other people is always, by definition, a moral issue, regardless of whether the actor chooses the proclivity to engage in it.

Berlin misleadingly talks about the involuntariness of being "sexually attracted to young people." The issue is not sexual attraction; it is sexual action. A healthy 20-year-old male with heterosexual interests is likely to be powerfully attracted to every halfway pretty woman he sees. This does not mean that he has, or attempts to have, sexual congress with these women, especially against their will. The entire psychiatric literature on what used to be called "sexual perversions" is permeated by the unfounded idea—always implied, sometimes asserted—that "abnormal" sexual impulses are harder to resist than "normal" ones.

The acceptance of this notion helps explain the widespread belief that sex offenders are more likely than other criminals to commit new crimes, an assumption that is not supported by the evidence. Tracking a sample of state prisoners who were released in 1983, the Bureau of Justice Statistics found that 52 percent of rapists and 48 percent of other sex offenders were arrested for a new crime within three years, compared to 60 percent of all violent offenders. The recidivism rates for nonviolent crimes were even higher: 70 percent for burglary and 78 percent for car theft, for example.

These numbers suggest that pedophiles resist their impulses more often than car thieves do. In any case, it is impossible to verify empirically whether an impulse is resistible. We can only say whether it was in fact resisted. But that doesn't matter, because the purpose of such a pseudo-medical claim is to excuse the actor of moral and legal responsibility.

Catholic officials took advantage of this psychiatric absolution to avoid dealing decisively with priests who were guilty of sexual abuse. What do church authorities do when a priest is accused of molesting children? They send him to a prestigious psychiatric hospital—Johns Hopkins in Baltimore, the Institute of Living in Hartford, the Menninger Foundation in Topeka—for "treatment." In practice, the psychiatric hospital is a safe house for the sexually misbehaving priest, a place where he can be hidden until he is quietly reassigned to continue his abuse elsewhere. Berlin claims such priests are closely watched after being discharged. But a priest who commits sexual abuse is a criminal who should be imprisoned, not a patient who should be monitored by psychiatrists in the church's pay.

The attitudes of ancient Greece

Sex with minors was not always considered a disease. In ancient Greece, sexual relationships between men and boys were a normal part of life. Such relations, called "pederastic," typically occurred between a 20-to-30-year-old man and a 12-to-17-year-old boy. The man pursued the boy, and the boy submitted to him as the passive partner in anal sex. The man also played the role of mentor to his pupil. With the arrival of heavy pubic hair, usually at age 18, the younger man found a boy to mentor and get sexual satisfaction from. Sexual relations between men and young children played no part in Greek pederasty. Judaism and Christianity redefined same-sex relations as unnatural and condemned them as sinful. Then, as criminal laws supplemented or replaced ecclesiastical laws, same-sex relations became crimes as well. That understanding governed popular opinion until the rise of secularism and medical science.

A priest who commits sexual abuse is a criminal who should be imprisoned, not a patient who should be monitored by psychiatrists in the church's pay.

The first person to propose redefining "pederasty," which in the 18th century became the term for what we call homosexuality, appears to have been the French physician Ambroise Tardieu (1818–1879). In 1857 Tardieu published a forensic-medical study to assist courts in cases involving pederasty. Tardieu believed that the penises of active homosexuals were anatomically different from the penises of passive homosexuals and "normal" men, that the anuses of passive homosexuals were anatomically different from the anuses of active homosexuals and normals, and that physicians could examine individuals and diagnose homosexuality by observing these alleged markers.

It remained for Karl Friedrich Otto Westphal (1833–1890), a famous German neurologist, to convert homosexuality from a disease identifiable by examining the subject's body into a mental illness identifiable by examining the subject's mind. Westphal renamed pederasty "sexual inversion" (in German, "contrary sexual feeling"), a term that was widely used well into the 20th century. It was also Westphal who popularized the erroneous idea, still held by many people, that male homosexuals are effeminate and female homosexuals are masculine. He argued that since sexual inversion was a disease it should be treated by doctors rather than punished by law.

A return to Athens

Creating diseases by coining pseudomedical terms was raised to the level of art by Baron Richard von Krafft-Ebing (1840–1902), a German-born professor of psychiatry at the Universities of Strasbourg, Graz, and Vienna. In his *Psychopathia Sexualis* (1886), which made him world famous, Krafft-Ebing authoritatively renamed sexual sins and crimes "sexual perversions" and declared them to be "cerebral neuroses." Lawyers, politicians, and the public embraced this transformation as the progress of science, instead of dismissing it as medical megalomania based on nothing more than the manipulation of language. "Sexology" became an integral part of medicine and the new science of psychiatry.

We have come a long way from Krafft-Ebing. In July 1998 Temple University psychologist Bruce Rind and two colleagues published their research on pedophilia in the *Psychological Bulletin,* a journal of the American Psychological Association. The authors concluded that the deleterious effects on a child of sexual relations with an adult "were neither pervasive nor typically intense." They recommended that a child's "willing encounter with positive reactions" be called "adult-child sex" instead of "abuse."

Not surprisingly, this conclusion created a furor, which led to a retraction and apology. Raymond Fowler, chief executive officer of the American Psychological Association, acknowledged that the journal's editors should have evaluated "the article based on its potential for misinforming the public policy process, but failed to do so."

Apparently no one noticed that, according to the fourth edition of the American Psychiatric Association's *Diagnostic and Statistical Manual of Mental Disorders* (*DSM-IV*, published in 1994), a person meets the criteria for pedophilia only if his "fantasies, sexual urges, or behaviors cause clinically significant distress or impairment in social, occupational, or other important areas of functioning." In short, pedophilia is a mental illness only if the actor is distressed by his actions. Psychiatrists had likewise classified homosexuality as a disease if the individual was dissatisfied with his sexual orientation ("ego-dystonic homosexuality"), but not if he was satisfied with it ("ego-syntonic homosexuality"). Bending to the wind, the American Psychiatric Association later backtracked. In *DSM-IV-TR*, published in 2000, the requirement of "clinically significant distress or impairment" was omitted from the criteria for pedophilia.

Mental health professionals are not the only "progressives" eager to legitimize adult-child sex by portraying opposition to it as old-fashioned antisexual prejudice. In a 1999 article, Harris Mirkin, a professor of political science at the University of Missouri-Kansas City, stated that "children are the last bastion of the old sexual morality." As summarized by *The New York Times,* he argued that "the notion of the innocent child was a social construct, that all intergenerational sex should not be lumped into one ugly pile and that the panic over pedophilia fit a pattern of public response to female sexuality and homosexuality, both of which were once considered deviant." Mirkin cited precedents such as Greek pederasty. "Though Americans consider intergenerational sex to be evil," he wrote, "it has been permissible or obligatory in many cultures and periods of history." He told the *Times:* "I don't think it's something where we should just clamp our heads in horror. . . . In 1900, everybody assumed that masturbation had grave physical consequences; that didn't make it true."

Because children cannot legally consent to anything, an adult using a child as a sexual object is engaging in a wrongful act.

The analogy is fatally flawed. Autoerotic acts differ radically from heteroerotic acts. Masturbation is something the child does for himself; it satisfies one of his biological urges. In that sense, masturbation is similar to urination or defecation. That is why we do not call masturbation a "sexual relationship," a term that implies the involvement of two (or more) persons, one of whom may be an involuntary participant. Masturbation (in private) is an amoral act: Strictly speaking, it falls outside the scope of moral considerations. In contrast, every sexual relationship is intrinsically a moral matter; medical (or pseudomedical-psychiatric) considerations ought to play no role in our judgments of such acts. The religiously enlightened person may view same-sex relations as evil. The psychologically enlightened person may view any consensual sex relations as good. Society must decide which sexual acts are permissible, and individuals must decide which sexual acts they condemn, condone, or wish to engage in.

The legal line

The criminal law defines sex between adults and minors as a crime. But the law is a blunt instrument. Technically, an 18-year-old male who has a consensual sexual relationship with a 17-year-old female is committing a criminal act (statutory rape), even though he might be only one day older than his partner. Such "crimes" generally are not prosecuted.

Sexual contact between a priest and a 10-year-old boy is quite another matter, and here is where the medicalization of unwanted or prohibited behaviors hinders our understanding. To impress the laity, physicians long ago took to using Greek and Latin words to describe diseases. For example, they called inflammation of the lung "pneumonia" and kidney failure "uremia." The result is that people now think that any Greco-Latin word ending in ia—or with the suffix philia or phobia—is a bona fide disease. This credulity would be humorous if it were not tragic.

Bibliophilia means the excessive love of books. It does not mean stealing books from libraries. Pedophilia means the excessive (sexual) love of children. It does not mean having sex with them, although that is what people generally have in mind when they use the term. Because children cannot legally consent to anything, an adult using a child as a sexual object is engaging in a wrongful act. Such an act is wrongful because it entails the use of physical coercion, the threat of such coercion, or (what comes to the same thing in a relationship between an adult and a child) the abuse of the adult's status as a trusted authority. The outcome of the act—whether it is beneficial or detrimental for the child—is irrelevant for judging its permissibility.

Saying that a priest who takes sexual advantage of a child entrusted to his care "suffers from pedophilia" implies that there is something wrong with his sexual functioning, just as saying that he suffers from pernicious anemia implies that there is something wrong with the functioning of his hematopoietic system. If that were the issue, it would be his problem, not ours. Our problem is that there is something wrong with him as a moral agent. We ought to focus on his immorality, and forget about his sexuality.

A priest who has sex with a child commits a grave moral wrong and also violates the criminal law. He does not treat himself as if he has a disease before he is apprehended, and we ought not to treat him that way afterward.

14

The Costs of Child Sexual Abuse Litigation Threaten the Catholic Church

Dan Michalski

Dan Michalski is a Dallas-based writer who has contributed to D *magazine,* Texas Monthly, *and the* London Observer.

Across America, Catholic dioceses are paying millions of dollars to victims of child sexual abuse at the hands of priests. As a result, the Catholic Church must face not only the tarnishing of its reputation because of child sexual abuse but the resulting financial damages as well. Cardinals are forced to lay off church employees, close offices, and shut down schools and seminaries to pay the high price of litigation. In addition to paying the victims of pedophile priests, some dioceses are paying for lawsuits that allege that church officials covered up the criminal acts of abusing priests. Some analysts argue that as a result of the high price of litigation, the Catholic Church has improved its handling of child sexual abuse by clergy. Others claim, however, that the problem has simply taught church officials better ways to "manage" rather than solve the problem.

R udy Kos, former Catholic priest and convicted molester of altar boys, just spent another hot summer in the unair-conditioned Texas prison where he is serving four life sentences for hundreds of incidents of sexual abuse of minors during the 1980s and early 1990s.

While Kos, 56, was hardly the first Catholic priest to sexually abuse a child, the court cases that have been brought against him since 1997 have made him one of the most significant. They set the precedent that the Catholic Church itself could be held financially responsible for the harm done by a rogue cleric's sins, bringing the issue of priestly pedophilia into a whole new world of punitive damages. A combination of a jury verdict and settlements in related civil suits required the Diocese of Dallas, where Kos had served as a pastor, to pay eleven victims $121 million, a record

Dan Michalski, "The Price of Priestly Prederasty," *Crisis*, vol. 19, October 2001, pp. 14–19. Copyright © 2001 by Crisis Magazine. Reproduced by permission.

sum that threatened to leave a flock of 415,000 Catholics virtually without a Church to shepherd it.

Attorneys for the former altar boys, now in their mid-20s and early 30s, convinced a jury that Bishop Charles Grahmann of Dallas and his predecessor, Bishop Thomas Tschoeppe, who headed the diocese when Kos committed the first of his crimes, and their hierarchy knew about Kos's abuse, did nothing to stop it, and then tried to cover it up.

A pattern of payouts

This pattern, we now know, would surface again and again in dioceses across the country as more cases of priestly pedophilia began to be filed. As of October 2001, more than 3,000 Catholic priests in America have been accused of sexual misconduct with minors, and nearly 2,000 insurance claims have been paid. (Kos is one of a few dozen priests to serve prison time.) Without exception, every one of the 188 dioceses in the American Catholic Church has faced or is facing claims of child sex abuse. Victims' organizations and others say the total payout has climbed past $1 billion, with another half-billion pending. Church officials insist the payout is far less, but they won't open their books to provide numbers. Regardless, the huge payments have come at a time when many dioceses find themselves already selling property, closing schools, and cutting programs in a fiscal crunch that coincides with smaller donations in the weekly collection baskets.

In August 2001, the Archdiocese of Los Angeles and the Diocese of Orange, California, agreed to pay $5.2 million to settle a lawsuit against a once-popular cleric, Monsignor Michael Harris, 56, alleged to have molested a high school boy in 1991, according to the Associated Press wire service. In July 2001, the *Boston Globe* reported that a judge had released the admission of Bernard Cardinal Law of the Archdiocese of Boston that he had known as early as 1984 about allegations of pederasty against John J. Geoghan, a since-defrocked priest who is the object of both a criminal prosecution and at least 84 civil suits over the alleged molestation of boys from 1962 to 1995. According to a lawyer for one of the alleged victims, Church documents reveal that Geoghan was removed from his parish but then assigned to another parish in 1985. The archdiocese has already paid millions of dollars in settlements in the Geoghan matter.

Rudy Kos, who went to prison in 1998, may be long gone from the Catholic scene—Pope John Paul II officially decreed his priestly ordination null and void—but the Church has been forever changed. If bishops seem as though they are putting lawyers' concerns above those of their own flocks, it is because sex-abuse scandals have ingrained a litigation mind-set into the culture of Church administration. No other organization, save maybe the tobacco companies, has seen liability lawsuits become such an integral part of its business. It is a transformation that is alienating priests who are guiltless of abuse and also many of their parishioners.

Laying down the law

In June 2001, Edward Cardinal Egan of New York called his archdiocesan priests to a special meeting at St. Joseph's Seminary in Yonkers. Hundreds of clergymen gathered to hear Cardinal Egan, along with a federal judge and an insurance industry representative, lay down the law regarding sexual abuse and misconduct among priests. An archdiocesan spokesman would not release a copy of the policies presented at the meeting or disclose in any specific detail what was discussed. But according to priests who were there, the cardinal's message was stern, solemn, and clear: This was still a very real problem, one the diocese could no longer afford.

"The two words he wanted us to leave with are 'Alert! Alert!'" one attendee, who did not wish to be identified, told the *New York Post.*

When then-Archbishop Egan (he was made a cardinal in February 2001) was appointed to succeed John Cardinal O'Connor, who died in May 2000, his first priority was to save the archdiocese from potential financial breakdown. New York had been operating for a decade with a $20 million budget deficit, and that didn't include individual parishes and schools that were also operating in the red. Cardinal Egan did not announce the details of his plan at the time, but rumors ran rampant through the chancery about what might be cut back. After little more than a year at the helm, he shut down more than a dozen church offices, laid off 26 employees, and closed two of New York's three seminaries. The politically influential archdiocesan newspaper, *Catholic New York,* survived Cardinal Egan's ax but was turned from a weekly into a monthly. He warned six schools that they might close, and in the end, three did, unable to raise funds to save themselves.

Without exception, every one of the 188 dioceses in the American Catholic Church has faced or is facing claims of child sex abuse.

At St. Anthony of Padua Church in the South Bronx, hundreds of parishioners gathered, some carrying signs, to plead with Cardinal Egan to save their schools and churches, many of which were on the chopping block because they had fallen into a costly state of disrepair. Sister Lucila Perez-Calixto of Instituto de Jeronimas de Puebla, in white habit and black veil, stood before the six-foot, four-inch archbishop pleading with him to save one of the poorest South Bronx churches, 131-year-old St. Jerome's. "They have nothing, absolutely nothing," she said. "Will you walk with us? Are you willing to help us? Come see our church and meet our people."

"Sister," he responded, "I have a question for you: If a piece of the ceiling falls down on this lady's head, will you assume the responsibility?" For Cardinal Egan, there was no escaping legal realities.

Officially, the Archdiocese of New York's fiscal woes have nothing to do with sex-abuse litigation. "They are not connected," insists spokesman Joe Zwilling. Asked how that could be possible, considering the number of new sexual malfeasance cases that are still being filed and the fact that insurance companies have set limits on what they will pay, he reiterates, "Because they are not connected."

But even as Cardinal Egan proceeds with his fiscal cleanup, the sex-abuse charges don't stop surfacing. Two of his priests were arrested in May

2001, one for allegedly soliciting sex over the Internet from an undercover FBI agent posing as a 14-year-old boy, the other for three years of alleged abuse in a parish rectory starting in 1998. Then in June 2001, less than two weeks after Cardinal Egan's meeting at the Yonkers seminary—where the cardinal reportedly demanded that archdiocesan priests report any evidence of clerical child molesting immediately and directly to him or his vicar—four priests in the Bronx were sued by a 21-year-old man who accused them of molesting him as a teenager and then roughing him up in an attempt to intimidate him so he wouldn't tell authorities.

The Dallas diocese had bluntly admitted that its $121 million liability in sexual abuse cases threatened to bankrupt it.

It is likely that Cardinal Egan learned some management lessons about dealing with such matters from his experience as the bishop of Bridgeport, Connecticut, before he arrived in New York. There, he was able to keep his diocese fiscally solvent in the face of dozens of molestation lawsuits. That meant closing some schools, consolidating others, and going through the same general downsizing process he is undertaking in New York. That doesn't mean the priestly pedophilia problem has been eradicated from his former see. In March 2001, when the Bridgeport diocese reportedly settled lawsuits involving six priests accused of molestation and 26 alleged victims for a relatively paltry $10 million, Cardinal Egan proved he knew how to keep the nine-figure lawsuits away.

Near-bankruptcy in Dallas

In 1999, the Dallas diocese had bluntly admitted that its $121 million liability in sexual abuse cases threatened to bankrupt it. The former altar boys and others who had brought the suits against Kos and two other Dallas priests also alleged to have molested minors said they didn't want to hurt the lay faithful of Dallas and eventually settled for around $31 million. After a legal battle with its insurance company over coverage, the Dallas chancery still found itself $11 million short. Land and other disposable assets were sold immediately and staff positions cut. Eventually, though, diocese officials had to consider closing schools.

The first school to be so threatened was St. Anne's, which had served a poor Mexican-American community for generations but which also happened to be situated on one and a quarter acres of prime real estate in the resurgent downtown Dallas arts district. That turned out to be a blessing in disguise. The diocese got its first good press in years, as the public generally sympathized with its plight: having to choose between shutting down the school or going to court to file for bankruptcy. In the end, the school would be saved—not by the diocese but by the city, which declared the 120-year-old building a historic landmark, meaning that it couldn't be torn down. The land underneath it was suddenly worth almost nothing.

Meanwhile, financial stresses were causing divisions in many parishes and schools all over the diocese. Documented in letters and reports by parish finance councils was a growing distrust of Church institutions, even when allegations of child molesting were not at issue. At All Saints Church in Dallas, where Kos and the two other alleged pedophile priests once served, the pastor, Monsignor Robert Rehkemper, insisted on building a school that 80 percent of the parish had voted against. "No one knew why the monsignor wanted it so bad, but he wasn't going to let the parish stop him," remembers David Bellavance, All Saints's lay finance administrator. "The numbers just didn't add up. We didn't know who we could trust."

Conspiracy theories abounded at All Saints: Parishioners attributed the pastor's decision to everything from an attempt to hide diocesan assets that would otherwise go to pay victims in the Kos cases to an aging monsignor's desire to see his name on a building somewhere in the diocese before he died. Bellavance, along with six others on the finance council, resigned and left the parish. He now worships at the Southern Methodist University Catholic student center in Dallas—which just had its budget slashed by the cash-strapped diocese. "We have 1,500 kids here who could really use some help," says Bellavance, who claims he is not surprised that students who generate little in donations to the diocese are seeing their funding cut. "We feel abandoned. But what can you do?"

The feeling that pedophilia has become as much of a financial crisis as a sexual one for the U.S. Catholic Church was reaffirmed in July 1999, when Bishop James Sullivan of Fargo, North Dakota, made diocesan employees sign a covenant saying they had not and would not commit a list of 14 specific sins. The list included pedophilia, exhibitionism, voyeurism, causing a pregnancy outside marriage, sexual harassment, and homosexuality, along with embezzlement and drunk driving. But the list didn't include other obviously immoral acts such as bank robbery and terrorism. It didn't take long for North Dakota Catholics to realize what these 14 sins were—all offenses for which the diocese, as an employer, could be sued. (Bishop Sullivan eventually withdrew the covenant after eight employees left their jobs, 18 hired lawyers to launch a legal challenge in protest, and four diocesan priests set up a legal defense fund to support the employees.)

A disaster in Santa Rosa

In July 1999, a lawsuit against the Diocese of Santa Rosa, California, would show Catholics how ugly—and expensive—sexual malfeasance in a church can get. Like other dioceses around the country, Santa Rosa had experienced a handful of costly sexual abuse lawsuits in the early and mid-1990s. By 1995, the settlements exceeded $5.4 million. In accordance with legal accords and as a long-awaited show of compassion, then-Bishop Patrick Ziemann pledged to pay for counseling for any person claiming to be molested by a clergyman. Five years later, records would show that Bishop Ziemann kept his promise. In 1995, he was spending about $1,000 a month for the psychological treatment of pedophilia victims. That amount would grow to $28,000 a month before another lawsuit forced him to resign from office.

This time it was a priest who signed on as plaintiff—and his alleged abuser was the bishop himself. The priest, who had just been accused of stealing money from collection plates, claimed that the bishop had black-mailed him for sex. The bishop at first denied any sexual relationship—until faced with DNA and taped evidence, at which point he insisted the sex between him and the young priest was consensual.

The revelation, followed by Bishop Ziemann's resignation a few days later, spurred the Vatican to send in Archbishop William Levada of San Francisco to survey and clean up the tawdry mess. In the months that followed, the public learned about a different kind of wrongdoing: On Bishop Ziemann's watch, the diocesan treasury had been raided. The chancery had covered these losses by dipping into millions of dollars in a consolidated fund used by parishes and other entities in the diocese. Money collected for school construction, parish maintenance, missions, and church charities was gone. The diocese had also stopped paying money into its pension funds for priests and lay employees. Some $16 million turned out to be missing—and that was on top of a $12.8 million budget deficit.

Sadly, and perhaps unfairly, sex scandals are now associated with the Catholic Church in the minds of many.

Furthermore, from 1995 to 1999, Bishop Ziemann's personal discretionary account had zoomed from $135,000 to nearly $2 million, with more than a quarter of that amount going to counseling costs for clerical sex abuse victims in Santa Rosa and elsewhere. That money was in addition to the $2 million the diocese had to pay to cover what insurance wouldn't in the 1995 settlements. It was now clear just how expensive priestly sex scandals could be. The cost would be felt by everyone in the diocese.

Questioning diocese policy

Parishioners from all over the diocese signed a letter to Archbishop Levada demanding "honesty at all levels, not spin control" in his handling of the Bishop Ziemann affair. Archbishop Levada seemed to comply to some degree. Members of one parish, St. Mary of the Angels in Ukiah, for example, learned that more than $1 million of their own church and school's savings had been wiped out. Archbishop Levada also revealed that Bishop Ziemann, along with the diocese's financial administrator, Monsignor Thomas Keys, had invested $5 million in a shady Luxembourg-based firm under investigation for fraud by the U.S. government, and that other diocesan money had gone into an illegal pyramid scheme.

With Bishop Ziemann now at a Pennsylvania treatment center while investigations into the charges against him continued, Archbishop Levada borrowed $6 million from his fellow California bishops to meet immediate operating expenses in Santa Rosa. He cut the chancery administrative staff in half, halted $12 million in building programs, and ended subsidies to parochial schools. "For Sale" signs went up in front of a diocesan retreat house and a 16-acre tract alongside the Cathedral of St. Eugene in Santa Rosa—land that had served as collateral for a $5 million dollar operating fund loan that Bishop Levada had taken out to meet expenses.

Many lay members of the diocese, in letters and at public meetings, demanded prison for Bishop Ziemann. But a five-month investigation by police ended with no criminal charges filed. Diocesan officials maintained that there was insufficient evidence to prosecute the bishop. But the Santa Rosa police chief, Michael Dunbaugh, disputed this: "The simple fact is that the diocese failed to cooperate fully." The district attorney, Mike Mullins, echoed this assertion, saying that diocesan authorities had told police they wanted to handle the Bishop Ziemann problem "internally."

One parish school threatened with closure was St. Bernard in Eureka. Its families managed, in just six months, to raise $1.6 million to keep its doors open. But that money came on the strict condition, set down by donors large and small alike, that none of the money be turned over to the diocesan office. That was a common sentiment around the Santa Rosa diocese, and St. Bernard's established a fund that allowed it to operate independently.

Many Santa Rosa priests felt both unjustly smeared with wrongdoing themselves and demoralized by the scandal and its fallout. Reverend Hans Ruygt, pastor of St. Mary of the Angels, for example, took medical leave after learning that his church had lost $1 million in the financial crisis. Father Ruygt "felt he just couldn't walk through town with his Roman collar on anymore," says another former Ukiah pastor, Reverend Gary Lombardi, whose own parish, St. Vincent Catholic Church, in Petaluma, California, lost $2.2 million.

A plague of scandals

Sadly, and perhaps unfairly, sex scandals are now associated with the Catholic Church in the minds of many. At least five U.S. bishops and archbishops resigned during the 1990s amid claims of illicit sex. Two cases involved affairs with women, two involved child molestation, and one, Bishop Ziemann's, involved an alleged affair with a priest. And the situation hardly seems to be improving. Catholics have seen at least two U.S. seminaries—St. Thomas's in Denver and St. Anthony's in Santa Barbara, California—closed at least partly because of reported sex between teachers and seminarians. The *Kansas City Star* reported in January 2000 that priests were dying of AIDS at four times the rate of the general U.S. population.

The Church is being needled on the sex-abuse front not just by lawyers but by grassroots lay Catholic groups.

The suits against Rudy Kos named not only the Dallas bishops, exposing the diocese itself to legal liability, but also the National Conference of Catholic Bishops (NCCB) and its political arm, the U.S. Catholic Conference (the two have recently merged into a single entity, the U.S. Conference of Catholic Bishops). The lawsuits contended that these national organizations oversaw a nationwide conspiracy of clerical sexual cover-up. The court, however, refused to extend the suit to the national bodies, partly because both held themselves out as mere consultative organizations that lacked supervisory power over individual bishops.

Nonetheless, an NCCB document distributed to every U.S. bishop in 1985 had forthrightly acknowledged that clerical pederasty was a widespread problem and proposed a plan for dealing with it that the bishops ultimately rejected. The existence of that secret, 92-page report—written by canon lawyer Reverend Thomas Doyle and Ray Mouton, the Church attorney in the first-ever multimillion-dollar priestly pedophilia lawsuit—convinced the Texas court that the Dallas bishops knew enough about the pedophilia crisis they were facing to justify holding the entire diocese liable in the Kos lawsuits. The document also asserted, "At the rate cases are developing, [losses of] $1 billion over 10 years is a conservative cost projection." That was in 1985, 16 years ago, before verdicts like the one in the Kos case were even imagined.

In many dioceses, priests say they have grown to expect the bishop to pay less attention to their concerns than to those of the Church's lawyers and insurance companies.

Now the Church is being needled on the sex-abuse front not just by lawyers but by grassroots lay Catholic groups. Clerical molestation victims first started organizing and collecting data and documents in Illinois after the Archdiocese of Chicago was hit with a rash of pedophilia suits and criminal prosecutions in the 1980s. In depositions in those suits, evidence surfaced that seemed to suggest that high Church officials were covering up their own sexual activities—hence the climate of secrecy. Stephen Brady was finally fed up, and in 1996, he formed a conservative watchdog group, Roman Catholic Faithful, Inc. (RCF), based in his hometown, Petersburg, Illinois, claiming that his own complaints about homosexual clerics typically fell on deaf ears. "If the bishops won't correct the problems, then the bishops need to be taken care of," Brady says, "exposed publicly, as the Scripture tells us, so the rest will fear."

He found many conservative priests who, feeling similarly squelched by an unsympathetic Church bureaucracy, were looking for a venue in which to express their own frustrations. They notified RCF of gay-priest Web sites, where content ranged from the disrespectful (calling Joseph Cardinal Ratzinger "Uncle Ratz") to the vulgar (graphic tips for oral sex). Brady printed the bulletin-board exchanges in his magazine, *Ad Majorem Dei Gloriam*. The publication often attempted to "out" allegedly gay priests and those affiliated with gay Catholic splinter groups such as Dignity/USA. Brady and his writers proffered theories about a "boys' club" of bishops that consisted primarily of once and future leaders of the NCCB.

One RCF target, Bishop Daniel Ryan of Springfield, Illinois, resigned in October 1999, a year before reaching the usual retirement age for bishops of 70, and a week before a still-pending civil lawsuit was filed against him alleging that he had failed to act against an alleged pedophile priest in his diocese because he himself was involved in homosexual misdeeds. Bishop Ryan denied the charges, and a diocesan spokesman told the local press that "there is no connection" between the bishop's resignation and the lawsuit.

Quick, quiet settlements

After a brief surge of openness following the Kos case, the U.S. Church has returned to handling sex abuse quietly and quickly, lawyers and victims say—although it is now the rule to suspend accused priests instead of simply moving them to a new parish. The Evanston Insurance Company (affiliated with Lloyds of London) now underwrites a policy specifically tailored to churches and clergy that covers "any act of unlawful sexual intimacy, sexual molestation or sexual assault" up to $1 million. That means dioceses can now obtain insurance, at a cost of about $2,500 per cleric per year, against criminal acts.

The standard operating procedure now is for dioceses to offer victims and their families cash up front, with their silence on the matter as a condition of the settlement. In addition, victims' groups with which the Church used to consult, such as Linkup and Survivors Network for Those Abused by Priests, say that the hierarchy has now cut off contact with them.

"Things have gotten better, and things have gotten worse," says Tom Economus, head of Linkup. "It's handled with a more caring hand now, but really, all they've figured out is how to manage the situation better."

Improving diocesan fiscal accountability—implementing measures that could have prevented the Santa Rosa fiasco—has been a recurring goal of the bishops' conference since as early as 1971. But despite work by a variety of ad hoc committees leading to new resolutions, the conference says it has found it difficult under canon law to force a bishop to perform an annual audit, let alone one signed off on by lay diocesan finance councils or released to the public. (And doing so could add a whole new level of liability to future molestation lawsuits.) While a unanimously approved resolution at the November 2000 bishops' meeting attempts to make individual bishops more financially accountable, ultimately, a conference spokesman admits, some diocesan bishops will end up essentially reporting only to themselves.

Because child sex abuse in the priesthood has proved to be so widespread, it has actually become easier for the Church to handle cases quietly. As the shock of contemplating a man in a Roman collar molesting a youth has diminished—and because legal documents related to such matters are more often than not sealed—new lawsuits get little attention from the press even when they are not quickly settled.

So where does that leave the good priests? They, too, have been tarnished by the unearthing of a sexual underworld among men of the cloth. Many say they now no longer feel comfortable simply giving hugs to children, and some say they worry that a single allegation against a priest, even if it's unfounded, can derail a career. And in many dioceses, priests say they have grown to expect the bishop to pay less attention to their concerns than to those of the Church's lawyers and insurance companies.

Of course, if the U.S. bishops can't help but see their priests as potential legal liabilities, it's only because—thanks to the dastardly stereotype created by the likes of Rudy Kos and more than 1,000 others—they no longer can afford not to.

15

A Victim Speaks Out

Craig Martin

Craig Martin was abused at age eleven by Father Joseph Heitzer, a priest at St. Peter's Church in Forest Lake, Minnesota. The following address was delivered before the U.S. Conference of Catholic Bishops, in Dallas, Texas, on June 13, 2002.

After years of hiding my anger and pain at being a victim of child sexual abuse at the hands of a priest, I have decided to reveal the problems encountered by victims like me when coming to terms with sexual victimization. Priests not only seduce their victims but also the victims' parents, so rather than blame the abuser, victims often blame their parents for failing to protect them. They also blame themselves, often developing low self-esteem and depression. Many turn to drugs and alcohol to numb the pain. Trying to hide their anguish, victims repress their feelings, some even their memories of abuse. Others develop unhealthy attitudes toward women and sex. Unfortunately, when victims finally choose to confront the church in order to heal, many are re-abused by the church, which often attacks the victims' credibility. If the Catholic Church really wants to help the victims of abusive priests, it should accept responsibility for the actions of its clergy and avoid litigation that re-abuses victims.

Good morning, my name is Craig Martin. My presence here today represents a stop in what has been a very difficult and long journey for me, my family and others who are close to me. I speak today for myself and no one else.

Before I begin I would like to speak directly to the media in attendance. Today is a very difficult day for me. I ask you to respect my privacy and my family's privacy and let my statement today speak for itself. I need time after this. There may come a time when I will tell more of my story, but today will not be it. Thank you for respecting my wishes.

I would like to take this opportunity to thank the Conference of Bishops for inviting me to share my story today. Although this is extremely difficult and scary for me to do, my greatest hope is that I will be able to help others by sharing my story.

The people who provide support

Before I begin, I would like to recognize three people:

- First, I'd like to recognize Father Kevin McDonough. Father Kevin, who I'll refer to simply as Kevin, is the Vicar General with the Archdiocese of Saint Paul and Minneapolis. Kevin has assisted me most in this journey when he has taken off his collar, stepped away from being a Church executive, and dealt with me person to person. I thank him for those times. However, those times where the Church has forced him to wear his collar are times that I have felt conflict and felt alone. Those are times where I do not feel as though my Church wants to help me down this very difficult path.

- Next, I'd like to recognize David Clohessy. David is executive director of SNAP—the Survivors Network of those Abused by Priests. He and his organization are very much needed. Survivors must be able to talk, to share, to rebuild, and to move forward. Thank you David and other survivors who have come forward to share their stories. Knowing that I am not alone provides comfort and hope for me. Thank you.

- I always save the best for last. I want to thank my best friend, my wife and my partner in this journey. Julie, thank you for your support and your love. I know that my pain at times has unfairly flowed into your life. Your faith sustains me, and it is the beacon that has helped lead me here today. Thank you. And I love you. . . .

The story of John Doe

Gentlemen, I wanted so desperately to be heard. I wanted someone to listen to me. I wanted someone to help me. I wanted to break the silence and despair that was killing me. I wanted someone to hear my story.

I find it easier to tell my story using the name John Doe. I can revisit my pain and not hurt myself again. I found many different stories that have helped me to understand my suffering. I will share some of those today so others can be helped.

In John's late twenties, he meets his future wife Julie. This is a start to his recovery, yet John has no idea. John's wife brings him back to religion and also introduces him to a priest that helps in John's recovery. I wish I could say recovery started here but John wasn't quite ready.

A *Sports Illustrated* article from September 13, 1999, entitled "Every Parent's Nightmare," best describes why John was in a position to be hurt.

"While society has no trouble envisioning the violent molester and the child who is forced to submit to a sexual predator, many people are baffled by how adult seducers are able to get [kids] to go along with them voluntarily. These men seduce children, in this case boys, in exactly the same way that men and women have been seducing each other since the dawn of mankind. In other words, they flirt with them, laugh at their jokes, and shower them with attention, with gifts, with affection. They size up their weaknesses, their vulnerabilities, their needs. They will target the kids who are more vulnerable."

The most amazing part of when I allowed John to talk about his abuser was how this man offered kindness and love; how this man became John's best friend. John showed very little anger toward his abuser. I was amazed at who John directed his sorrow to. He directed his sorrow not at his abuser, but at his parents. John tells a story of how his abuser wants to take John fishing. The abuser asks John's parents if it is OK. John's parents thought it was a great idea for John to go on a fishing trip with this Catholic priest. John talks of how his relationship with his parents changed, how he no longer trusted them. He feels he is alone.

Mom and Dad, I am terribly sorry for how I have treated you. I now know that I only have love in my heart for both of you.

The abused child

A child who is being abused is put in a frightening and confusing situation. They may never have heard of anything like this happening. Nobody has told them it is right, but nobody has told them it is wrong. Everyone may like and respect the person who is doing these things (*Surviving Childhood Sexual Abuse,* p. 57).

John remembers the motel that night with the priest, but hardly anything else. John has no idea how he got home. It is only 35 years later that John is starting to remember that horrible night.

Abused children often hide their anger and distress from other people so that no one will suspect that they are being abused. They may also keep their feelings under control while they are being abused to protect themselves from feeling distress and pain or because they do not want the abuser to see how much he is hurting them. Many adult survivors continue to cope by blocking feelings and trying to forget about the abuse (*Surviving Childhood Sexual Abuse,* p. 87).

Survivors often have a low opinion of themselves and lack self-confidence and self-esteem. They may feel worthless, useless and unlovable. Many survivors put on a "front" and present themselves as capable, cheerful and confident, while feeling wretched inside. Survivors may be so overwhelmed by their low opinion of themselves and lack of confidence that they may suffer bouts of depression, making them unable to act positively or find pleasure in things (*Surviving Childhood Sexual Abuse,* p. 116).

These words exactly describe John's feelings about his experience. John had become sexually active shortly after his abuse. John describes some very unhealthy attitudes toward women and admits to seeking out women in a predatory way. Alcohol also started to control John's life. It was many years before he finally sought help for alcoholism. Although sexual compulsivity and alcoholism had major effects on John, it was his need for self-esteem that kept him alive. John still admits today of having low self-esteem. John has shown symptoms of low self-esteem, depression, anger and the need to control. John has been able to survive, however, with the help of his wife, children and therapy.

The healing journey

Wendy Maltz, in her book, *The Sexual Healing Journey,* has these words for John Doe. "Begin your journey only when you feel ready for it. Go slowly. Pace yourself. Trust yourself. Remember: This is your journey." These words help John Doe start peeling back the onion. This phrase applies to the layers of destructive behavior most people acquire to save their life. Many of these coping skills become very addictive by nature as they did for John Doe.

I wanted someone to listen to me. I wanted someone to help me. I wanted to break the silence and despair that was killing me.

Many times people like John Doe must reach a low point in their lives before they can ask for help. John found that the pain was so intense in his life that the fear of being retraumatized was less threatening. Through organizations such as SNAP and other information resources, John has found out that he is not alone and has found ways to heal many different aspects of his life. Individual or group therapy is very important in John's life. Journaling is also a healthy way to confront the secrets of abuse as are 12-step programs, which John adheres to.

The secretive nature of male abuse has limited research. It is only recently that men have begun to seek help for sexual abuse. Since most men have ignored or have been unable to relate to their own abuse, this further hinders research. This situation of secrecy, coupled with Post Traumatic Stress Disorder, has caused considerable problems for the reconciliation between the John Does and the Catholic Church.

The re-abuse of victims

Following are excerpts from a research paper I wrote for a class at St. Cloud State University.

Exploring the steps taken by the Catholic Church in dealing with people like John Doe, I have found great discrepancies between Church and State. While the St. Paul-Minneapolis Archdiocese has made strides in the area of sexual abuse, I still have grave concerns about the Church.

I feel that the Church has decided the rules and how the game is to be played. I feel that the Church has shown its need for power with the court cases involving people who have been hurt by clergy. This is where the conflict between Church and state exists. The Catholic Church hides behind its lawyers and legal rights. The Church also tries to avoid damages caused by its own clergy. Finally, the Church wants authority to heal its own members and then make payments as to what they feel is appropriate to John Doe.

I'd like to read an excerpt from *Time* magazine to help people understand why this is more than just a physical violation of a child by a priest.

> For years most cases that made it to trial were civil com-
> plaints, but they were financially devastating, sometimes
> costing millions. Some dioceses adopted hardball legal tac-
> tics that abused victims all over again. Church lawyers attack
> the victims' credibility and besmirch their families. They
> bombard victims with as many as 500 written questions, de-
> mand 30 years' worth of tax returns, require names and
> dates for every doctor visited to age 12. They cross-examine
> mothers about their children's sex lives. As victim Lee White
> says, "It's intimidation, I feel like I'm being re-abused."

Father Kevin McDonough and others recommend reconciliation ver-
sus litigation, yet which one is protecting John Doe and which one is protecting the Church?

The Church cannot wear both hats into the arena of sexual offenders
and try to heal those who have been abused because of such actions. The
Church must acknowledge the magnitude of the damages.

Taking steps toward accountability

Acknowledgement by the Church might be the first step that needs to be
taken for people like John Doe to start their recovery process. A major issue facing the Catholic Church is the fact that it has tried to handle this
problem internally for so long. This has only increased the secrecy and
helped the Church continue to have control over those who have been
hurt. Is the Church willing or able to give that type of power back to
those who have been traumatized?

The Church must establish an independent resource for the healing
of both victims and offenders. The health community, law enforcement
agencies, and social service agencies can provide this service. Social workers can help in starting and continuing the healing process. Health professionals can administer necessary programs, and law enforcement can
protect and enforce the rights of all parties involved. I feel that it is essential to people like John Doe that the Church be responsible for the actions of its employees.

In regard to any financial settlements, I feel that it is vital for the
Church and John Doe to avoid litigation. This scenario will only retrau-
matize John and cause additional conflict among the members of the
Church. These members are essential for stewardship and the funds
needed to provide for the programs necessary to help all parties involved
to recover. I would hope that a trust fund can be provided by the Church
to establish the monies needed. An administrative board could handle
these funds, with all concerned parties having access to the funds. A need
basis account could be established for emergency situations. Establish-
ment of this fund would extract some of the Church's power and show
responsibility on the part of the Church.

In closing, I ask, "Can the Catholic Church respond in such a way to
end harm caused by its employees?" I firmly believe it can. You see, I am
John Doe. I have made progress in my recovery and the Church has played
a role in that. It's with my personal experiences that I can understand the

pain and suffering of all those involved. I'm committed to helping other John Does and to helping the Church in finding solutions to an enormous problem. I can only hope and pray that the Catholic Church will find the way to admit its wrongs, ask for forgiveness from every person from every walk of life, and help them successfully continue their journey.

Thank you very much.

16

A Nonabusing Priest Speaks Out

J. Ronald Knott

J. Ronald Knott is a priest of the archdiocese of Louisville, Kentucky, and is vocation director and director of Catholic worship at Bellarmine University in Louisville.

The scandal of child sexual abuse in the Catholic Church has made it hard for nonabusing priests who have given everything to their profession. They suffer the pain of all who have been hurt by the scandal, from the victims and their families to the abusive priests and well-meaning bishops. What is most difficult, however, is the self-doubt that arises in the hearts of innocent priests. However, hope comes from preaching to those Catholics who have not lost faith. Their support and encouragement teaches that rewards come to those who are strong when facing a crisis.

In my 32 years as a priest, I have been threatened by the Ku Klux Klan, have been thrown out of a ministerial association because I am a Catholic, have had fundamentalist preachers run me down by name on the radio and have had a knife pulled on me in church for a homily I gave. I have also seen one of my rectory mates carted off for alcohol addiction and another leave the priesthood. I have been stalked by a schizophrenic and singled out in a hateful crusade by right-wing Catholics because I welcomed marginal Catholics. While I was serving as its pastor, the cathedral walls cracked down the back and along one side and almost fell to the ground two-thirds of the way into a renovation. Finally, I have had my house broken into three times.

A bleeding heart

Nothing, however, has affected me like this damnable sex scandal the church in the United States is going through right now. I am at the lowest point I have reached in 32 years. In response, I have done predictable things, like "isolating" myself. A few weeks ago, however, I did something that I have never done before. I was driving somewhere wearing my Roman collar. When I pulled up to a light, I put my hand over the collar so that the people on each side would not see it. In the latest of three nightmares, I dreamed I was back in the seminary when the police came and took everything I owned; my books, my homily collection, my spiritual journals, my clothes, my family photos, my money, everything! My heart is obviously bleeding from many holes.

In the first place, my heart bleeds for the victims and their families. As a person who was psychologically abused throughout childhood, I know a little about that particular brand of abuse and how it can destroy one's self-image, how one can blame oneself, how toxic anger can be stifled and how powerless one can feel. It took me 21 years even to begin coming to grips with the sort of abuse I experienced and even longer to forgive the one who inflicted it. That took years of intense inner work. I can only imagine how devastating sexual abuse must be.

My heart bleeds for all those faithful Catholics who have been scandalized and have had their faith shaken.

Yet my heart also bleeds for the abusing priests. Yes, I have compassion, even for them. I cannot imagine the humiliation they must feel, many of them now in their old age. While in no way would I minimize the damage they have caused, I struggle with an effort to reconcile the large spark of goodness in these men with the evil they have done. I suppose I could hate them, if I knew what their victims know, but I did not know that side of them. I knew another man, and that man was kind, generous, hard working and dedicated. I suppose the key to reconciling those opposites is indicated in the old adage, "Love the sinner and hate the sin."

In the third place, my heart bleeds for all those faithful Catholics who have been scandalized and have had their faith shaken, a faith that is hard to hold on to these days in any case. My heart bleeds for all those angry and alienated Catholics who see in these events even more reason to be angry and alienated. As one who has specialized in trying to clear a path for the return of alienated people, I know that such a trip home has now become even more difficult, if not more unlikely.

And then my heart bleeds for those faithful priests who have to bear the shame brought on a profession they love, a profession to which they have given their all. As a vocation director, I find that a hard job suddenly seems impossible. My aim is to present the priesthood to young people as a chance to "do something beautiful for the Lord," something that I have enjoyed doing even when the pickings were slim. Now I feel as though I came home one day to find that my priceless Renoir had been clawed to shreds by cats. This has left me with a sick feeling in my guts. It reminds me that thousands of great nuns, the majority of whom were even heroic, have experienced similar unfairness. They have been stereotyped by endless jokes in movies, plays and stand-up comedy about a few cruel and heartless nuns in the classrooms of the past. Indeed, a few bad apples can spoil the barrel.

In the fifth place, my heart bleeds for the bishops, even for those who should have known better. After having lived with one bishop for 14 years, I know how impossible a bishop's job can often be. Thirty or 40 years ago, most bishops did not know enough about the problem of sexual abuse of children to know what to do. They did what most families did with unwed pregnancies. They kept it quiet. Fifteen years ago, many bishops were given bad advice by "professionals" who told them that therapy and counseling worked and their clients could safely return to ministry. Bishops have also had to make their way across the alligator swamp of insurance companies and lawyers and the media. What was considered good advice yesterday is indicted as a coverup today.

From self-doubt to hope

Last of all, my heart bleeds for priests like myself who have been thrown into a whirlpool of self-doubt, especially when the pope recently told a group of the newly ordained that they "must be perfect." It has taken me 35 years to quit beating myself up for not being perfect and to accept the consolation that my best is good enough for God. Now we priests are sitting around rectories, homes and apartments combing through our lives for every thought, word or deed, for every youthful indiscretion, every joke, every hug, every touch, that could come home to haunt us. Not one of us has failed to have the chilling thought of being falsely accused as the late Cardinal Joseph Bernardin of Chicago once was and as Cardinal Roger Mahony of Los Angeles has recently been. We know that if we are falsely charged we might as well be guilty, because once accused, we would never fully recover our reputations. I am sad to say that I don't know any priest who is now completely at ease around children.

I am sad to say that I don't know any priest who is now completely at ease around children.

Yes, I have been tempted in the last few weeks to hide my collar and quit my job as a vocation director, but I have also felt a surge of hope. Like Jonah (2:8), "when my soul fainted within me, I remembered the Lord." Like Jeremiah (20:9), I have been tempted "not to think about him, not to speak his name any more. Then there seemed to be a fire burning in my heart, imprisoned in my bones. The effort to restrain it wearied me; I could not bear it."

My source of hope comes from the pews, when I "share the Scriptures" and "break the bread" with faithful Catholics who have taught me once again that their faith is solidly rooted. That faith is not, nor has it ever been, in God's weak messengers, but in the sacred message they proclaim. St. Paul says that we are all "earthenware jars that hold a great treasure." Everywhere around the country, faithful Catholics seem to know the difference between the treasure and the crock. They have reminded me once again that the validity of the Gospel does not depend on the personal goodness of the messenger. They know that most of us are doing the best we can, often trying to lead two and three parishes or fulfill multiple ministries while holding ourselves together at the same time. They know we need their support and encouragement, especially during these trying times, and they give it freely. I am one very thankful recipient of that support and encouragement.

My fellow Catholics wish for me what Paul wished for Timothy when the latter was discouraged enough to quit: sophronismos. That is a nearly untranslatable word that means "knowing how to act in the face of panic" (2 Tim. 1:7).

Organizations to Contact

The editors have compiled the following list of organizations concerned with the issues debated in this book. The descriptions are derived from materials provided by the organizations. All have publications or information available for interested readers. The list was compiled on the date of publication of the present volume; names, addresses, phone and fax numbers, and e-mail and Internet addresses may change. Be aware that many organizations take several weeks or longer to respond to inquiries, so allow as much time as possible.

ACT for Kids
7 S. Howard, Suite 200, Spokane, WA 99201-3816
(866) 348-5437 • fax: (509) 747-0609
e-mail: resources@actforkids.org • website: www.actforkids.org

ACT for Kids is a nonprofit organization that provides resources, consultation, research, and training for the prevention and treatment of child abuse and sexual violence. The organization publishes workbooks, manuals, and books such as *He Told Me Not to Tell* and *How to Survive the Sexual Abuse of Your Child.*

American Academy of Child and Adolescent Psychiatry (AACAP)
3615 Wisconsin Ave. NW, Washington, DC 20016-3007
(202) 966-7300 • fax: (202) 966-2891
website: www.aacap.org

AACAP is a nonprofit organization that supports and advances child and adolescent psychiatry through research and the distribution of information. The academy's goal is to provide information that will remove the stigma associated with mental illnesses and assure proper treatment for children who suffer from mental or behavioral disorders due to child abuse, molestation, or other factors. AACAP publishes "Facts for Families" on a variety of issues concerning disorders that may affect children and adolescents. Titles include "Child Sexual Abuse" and "Responding to Child Sexual Abuse."

American Professional Society on the Abuse of Children (APSAC)
940 NE 13th St., Oklahoma City, OK 73104
(405) 271-8202 • fax: (405) 271-2931
e-mail: tricia-williams@ouhsc.edu • website: www.apsac.org

The APSAC is dedicated to improving the coordination of services in the fields of child abuse prevention, treatment, and research. It publishes a quarterly newsletter, the *Advisor,* and the *Journal of Interpersonal Violence.*

Association for the Rights of Catholics in the Church (ARCC)
PO Box 85, Southampton, MA 01073
(413) 527-9929 • fax: (413) 527-5877
e-mail: arccangel@charter.net • website: http://arcc-catholic-rights.org

Founded in 1980 by lay and clerical Catholics, ARCC's primary goal is to promote accountability, institutionalize shared decision making, and preserve the rights of all Catholics. On its website, ARCC provides access to archives of its newsletter, the *ARCC Light*, and documents written by ARCC members, including "Vatican Must Deal Openly with Priest Pedophilia Cases."

Association for the Treatment of Sexual Abuse (ATSA)
4900 SW Griffith Dr., Suite 274, Beaverton, OR 97005
(503) 643-1023 • fax: (503) 643-5084
e-mail: igrid@atsa.com • website: www.atsa.com

To eliminate sexual victimization and protect communities from sex offenders, ATSA fosters research, furthers professional education, and advances professional standards and practices in the field of sex offender evaluation and treatment. The association publishes the quarterly *ATSA Journal*. The ATSA website features links to other organizations and access to current research and conferences.

Call to Action USA (CTA)
2135 W. Roscoe, Chicago, IL 60618
(773) 404-0004 • fax: (773) 404-1610
e-mail: cta@cta-usa.org • website: www.cta-usa.org

CTA is a national organization that believes the spirit of God is at work among all in the Catholic Church, not just in its appointed leaders. CTA publishes *Call to Action News*, its newsletter covering developments in the church, and *Church Watch*, a progress report on reforms. On its website, CTA provides access to current and past issues of its publications and maintains updates and breaking news on current issues including the child sexual abuse crisis.

Canadian Society for the Investigation of Child Abuse (CSICA)
PO Box 42066, Acadia Postal Outlet, Calgary, Alberta, Canada T2J 7A6
(403) 289-8385
e-mail: info@csica.zener.com • website: www.csica.zener.com

CSICA is a nonprofit society formed to provide a coordinated, professional approach to child sexual abuse investigations. The society presents seminars and workshops on child sexual abuse and trains investigators. CSICA also responds to the needs of abused children. By teaching children about the courtroom and court processes, CSICA's programs enhance the judicial process and reduce the emotional trauma experienced by children in delivering their testimony in court. On its website, CSICA provides access to court preparation training materials, and a children's video and comic book, *You're Not Alone*, in which children share their courtroom experiences.

Center for the Prevention of Sexual and Domestic Violence (CPSDV)
2400 N. 45th St., #10, Seattle, WA 98103
(206) 634-1903 • fax: (206) 634-0115
e-mail: cpsdv@cpsdv.org • website: www.cpsdv.org

The center serves as an interreligious educational resource addressing issues of sexual and domestic violence. The goal of CPSDV is to assist religious leaders in the task of ending abuse. The center publishes books and videos on sexual abuse by clergy and *Working Together*, a quarterly newsletter that includes articles, editorials, book reviews, resources, and information about local, national, and international prevention efforts. The CPSDV website provides resources on sexual abuse by clergy, including "Gay Priests: The Catholic Church's Red Herring" and "Confidentiality and Mandatory Reporting: A Clergy Dilemma?"

Child Welfare League of America (CWLA)
440 First St. NW, Third Floor, Washington, DC 20001-2085
(202) 638-2952 • fax: (202) 638-4004
website: www.cwla.org

The Child Welfare League of America is an association of more than seven hundred public and private agencies and organizations devoted to improving the lives of children. CWLA publications include the book *Tender Mercies: Inside the World of a Child Abuse Investigator*, the quarterly magazine *Children's Voice*, and the bimonthly journal *Child Welfare*.

False Memory Syndrome Foundation
1955 Locust St., Philadelphia, PA 19103-5766
(215) 940-1040 • fax: (215) 940-1042
e-mail: mail@fmsfonline.org • website: www.fmsfonline.org/index.html

The foundation believes that many "delayed memories" of sexual abuse are the result of false memory syndrome (FMS). In FMS, patients in therapy "recall" childhood abuse that never occurred. The foundation seeks to discover reasons for the spread of FMS, works for the prevention of new cases, and aids FMS victims, including those falsely accused of abuse. The foundation publishes a newsletter and various papers and distributes articles and information on FMS.

Interfaith Sexual Trauma Institute (ISTI)
Saint John's Abbey and University, Collegeville, MN 56321
e-mail: isti@csbsju-edu • website: www.csbsju.edu/isti

To facilitate safe, healthy, and trustworthy communities of faith, ISTI promotes the prevention of sexual abuse, exploitation, and harassment through research, education, and publication. The institute facilitates healing for survivors, communities of faith, and offenders. The institute publishes books, including *Before the Fall: Preventing Pastoral Sexual Abuse* and *Recovering the Lost Self: Shame Healing for Victims of Clergy Sexual Abuse*, and the *ISTI Sun* newsletter, including articles such as "Abuse of Power, Part I and II," available on its website.

Kempe Children's Center
1825 Marion St., Denver, CO 80218
(303) 864-5252 • fax: (303) 864-5302
e-mail: Kempe@KempeCenter.org • website: www.kempecenter.org

The Kempe Children's Center, formerly the C. Henry Kempe National Center for the Prevention and Treatment of Child Abuse and Neglect, is a resource for research on all forms of child abuse and neglect. It is committed to multidisciplinary approaches to improve recognition, treatment, and prevention of abuse. The center's resource library offers a catalog of books, booklets, information packets, and articles on child sexual abuse issues.

Klaas Kids Foundation
PO Box 925, Sausalito, CA 94966
(415) 331-6867 • fax: (415) 331-5633
e-mail: klaaskids@pacbell.net • website: www.klaaskids.org

The Klaas Kids Foundation was established in 1994 after the death of twelve-year-old kidnap and murder victim Polly Hannah Klaas. The foundation's goals are to acknowledge that crimes against children deserve a high priority and to form partnerships with concerned citizens, the private sector, organizations, law enforcement, and legislators to fight crimes against children. The foundation publishes a quarterly newsletter, the *Klaas Action Review*.

The Linkup
118 Chestnut St., Cloverport, KY 40111
(270) 788-6924
e-mail: ILINKUP@aol.com • website: www.thelinkup.com

The primary goal of The Linkup is to prevent clergy abuse and to empower and assist its victims to overcome its traumatic effects on their lives. The Linkup also encourages religious institutions to develop and implement responsible, accountable policies and procedures. On its website, the *Missing Link Online*, The Linkup publishes news and articles.

Male Survivor
5505 Connecticut Ave. NW, Washington, DC 20015-2601
(800) 738-4181
website: www.malesurvivor.org

Male Survivor, formerly National Organization on Male Sexual Victimization (NOMSV), believes that sexually victimized boys and men need added support to come forward and ask for help. Identification, assessment, and intervention help prevent abused boys from becoming self-destructive or abusive adolescents and men. The organization, which respects the diversity of sexual abuse survivors, serves anyone who has been sexually abused. Male Survivor helps the public and the media to recognize and understand males who have been sexually abused and promotes action to confront and fight male sexual abuse. The Male Survivor website provides information for survivors, clinicians, and caregivers. It also provides access to news and *Male Survivor*, its quarterly newsletter.

National Association of State VOCAL Organizations (NASVO)
PO Box 1314, Orangevale, CA 95662
(800) 745-8778 • (916) 863-7470
website: www.nasvo.org

The National Association of State Victims of Child Abuse Laws (VOCAL) Organizations provides information and data, conducts research, and offers emotional support for those who have been falsely accused of child abuse. NASVO maintains a library of research on child abuse and neglect issues, focusing on legal, mental health, social, and medical issues, and will provide photocopies of articles for a fee. It publishes the bimonthly newsletter *NASVO News*.

National Center for Missing and Exploited Children (NCMEC)
699 Prince St., Alexandria, VA 22314
(800) THE LOST • (703) 739-0321
website: www.missingkids.com

The NCMEC serves as a clearinghouse of information on missing and exploited children and coordinates child protection efforts with the private sector. A number of publications on these issues are available, including guidelines for parents whose children are testifying in court, help for abused children, and booklets such as *Child Molesters: A Behavioral Analysis* and *How to Keep Your Child Safe: A Message to Every Parent*.

National Center for Prosecution of Child Abuse
American Prosecutors Research Institute
99 Canal Center Plaza, Suite 510, Alexandria, VA 22314
(703) 549-9222 • fax: (703) 836-3195
e-mail: ncpca@ndaa-apri.org
website: www.ndaa-apri.org/apri/programs/ncpca/index.html

The center seeks to improve the investigation and prosecution of child abuse cases. A clearinghouse on child abuse laws and court reforms, the center supports research on reducing courtroom trauma for child victims. It publishes a monthly newsletter, *Update*, as well as monographs, bibliographies, special reports, and a manual for prosecutors, *Investigation and Prosecution of Child Abuse.*

National Clearinghouse on Child Abuse and Neglect Information
330 C St. SW, Washington, DC 20447
(703) 385-7565 • (800) 394-3366 • fax: (703) 385-3206
e-mail: nccanch@calib.com • website: www.calib.com/nccanch

This national clearinghouse collects, catalogs, and disseminates information on all aspects of child maltreatment, including identification, prevention, treatment, public awareness, training, and education. The clearinghouse offers various reports, fact sheets, and bulletins concerning child abuse and neglect.

Quixote Center
PO Box 5206, Hyattsville, MD 02782
(301) 699-0042 • fax: (301) 864-2182
e-mail: Quixote@quixote.org • website: www.quixote.org

The goal of the Quixote Center is to make the Catholic Church more just, peaceful, and equitable in its policies and practices. The Catholics Speak Out project of the Quixote Center encourages reform in the Roman Catholic Church. The project works toward equality and justice within the church and dialogue between the laity and hierarchy on issues of sexuality, sexual orientation, and reproduction. On its website, the center provides access to press releases and current issues of *Speaking Out,* the newsletter of Catholics Speak Out.

The Safer Society Foundation
PO Box 340-1, Brandon, VT 05733-0340
(802) 247-3132 • fax: (802) 247-4233
website: www.safersociety.org

The Safer Society Foundation is a national research, advocacy, and referral center for the prevention of sexual abuse of children and adults. The Safer Society Press publishes studies and books on the prevention of sexual abuse and on treatment for sexual abuse victims and offenders, including *Back on Track: Boys Dealing with Sexual Abuse.*

Survivors Network of Those Abused by Priests (SNAP)
PO Box 6416, Chicago, IL 60680
(312) 409-2720
website: www.survivorsnetwork.org

SNAP provides support for men and women who have been sexually abused by any clergy, including priests, brothers, nuns, deacons, and teachers. The network provides an extensive phone network, advocacy, information, and referrals. On its website, SNAP provides access to stories, statements, and speeches from survivors, a discussion board, news, and information on legal issues.

Voice of the Faithful (VOTF)
PO Box 423, Newton Upper Falls, MA 02464
(617) 558-5252
website: www.votf.org

VOTF is a lay group formed in response to the 2002 clergy sexual abuse crisis with the aim of restoring trust between the Catholic laity and hierarchy and rebuilding the Catholic Church. The organization supports survivors and "priests of integrity" and promotes Church reform that involves the laity in church governance. The VOTF website provides access to survivor and clergy support services and statements and articles on the child sexual abuse crisis.

Bibliography

Books

Candace Reed Benyei — *Understanding Clergy Misconduct in Religious Systems: Scapegoating, Family Secrets, and the Abuse of Power.* Binghamton, NY: Haworth, 1998.

Jason Berry and Andrew M. Greeley — *Lead Us Not into Temptation: Catholic Priests and the Sexual Abuse of Children.* Champaign: University of Illinois Press, 2000.

Boston Globe — *Betrayal: The Crisis in the Catholic Church.* Boston: Little, Brown, 2002.

Frank Bruni and Elinor Burkett — *A Gospel of Shame: Children, Sexual Abuse, and the Catholic Church.* New York: HarperPerennial, 2002.

Donald B. Cozzens — *The Changing Face of the Priesthood: A Reflection on the Priestly Crisis of Soul.* Collegeville, MN: Liturgical Press, 2000.

Donald B. Cozzens — *Sacred Silence: Denial and the Crisis in the Church.* Collegeville, MN: Liturgical Press, 2002.

Catherine Britton Fairbanks — *Hiding Behind the Collar.* Frederick, MD: Publish America, 2002.

Richard B. Gartner — *Betrayed as Boys: Psychodynamic Treatment of Sexually Abused Men.* New York: Guildford Press, 1999.

Healing Woman Foundation — *The Healing Journal: The International Journal for Survivors of Childhood Sexual Abuse.* Baltimore: Sidran, 2002.

Philip Jenkins — *Moral Panic: Changing Concepts of the Child Molester in Modern America.* New Haven, CT: Yale University Press, 1998.

Philip Jenkins — *Pedophiles and Priests: Anatomy of a Contemporary Crisis.* New York: Oxford University Press, 1996.

Eugene Kennedy — *The Unhealed Wound: The Church and Human Sexuality,* New York: St. Martin's Press, 2001.

James R. Kincaid — *Erotic Innocence: The Culture of Child Molesting.* Durham, NC: Duke University Press, 1998.

Thomas G. Plante, ed. — *Bless Me Father for I Have Sinned: Perspectives on Sexual Abuse Committed by Roman Catholic Priests.* Westport, CT: Praeger, 1999.

Michael S. Rose — *Goodbye, Good Men: How Liberals Brought Corruption into the Catholic Church.* Washington, DC: Regnery, 2002.

Stephen J. Rossetti — *A Tragic Grace: The Catholic Church and Child Sexual Abuse.* Collegeville, MN: Liturgical Press, 1996.

Diana E.H. Russell	*The Epidemic of Rape and Child Sexual Abuse in the United States.* Thousand Oaks, CA: Sage Publications, 2000.
A.W. Richard Sipe	*Celibacy: A Way of Loving, Living, and Serving.* Chicago: Triumph Books, 1996.

Periodicals

Sandra G. Boodman	"For Experts on Abuse, Priests' Orientation Isn't the Issue," *Washington Post,* June 24, 2002.
Vern L. Bullough	"Priests Are Human, and Sexual Too," *Free Inquiry,* Winter 2000.
William Byron	"Thinking Systemically: Church in Crisis," *Origins,* May 16, 2002.
Linda Chavez	"Change American Culture, Not the Church," *Conservative Chronicle,* May 1, 2002.
Richard Dawkins	"Religion's Real Child Abuse," *Free Inquiry,* Fall 2002.
Gill Donovan	"Some See Big Reforms on Horizon: Conservatives and Liberals Align in Call for Lay Involvement," *National Catholic Reporter,* July 19, 2002.
Mary Eberstadt	"The Elephant in the Sacristy," *Weekly Standard,* June 17, 2002.
G. Thomas Fitzpatrick	"Understanding the Pedophilia Crisis in the Boston Priesthood," *New Oxford Review,* June 2002.
John Gallagher	"The Shame of Father Shanley," *Advocate,* July 23, 2002.
Jennifer G. Hickey	"Church Explores 'Hard Change,'" *Insight,* August 12, 2002.
Michael W. Higgins	"The Church Must Change: A Canadian Expert on the Vatican Examines the Sex Abuse Scandal," *Maclean's,* May 13, 2002.
John F. Kavanaugh	"Abusing the Truth," *America,* May 27, 2002.
Eugene Kennedy	"Confessions of a Former Celibate," *Salon,* March 16, 2002.
Eugene Kennedy	"The Secret Cause of the Sex Abuse Scandal," *National Catholic Reporter,* June 11, 2002.
Bernard Law	"The Necessary Dimensions of a Sexual Abuse Policy," *Origins,* April 25, 2002.
John Leo	"Battle over Priests Could Result in Revolution," *Conservative Chronicle,* April 3, 2002.
John Leo	"A Gay Culture in the Church," *U.S. News & World Report,* June 3, 2002.
National Catholic Reporter	"Sex Offense: One Part of His Story," June 7, 2002.
Richard John Neuhaus	"Scandal Time III," *First Things,* August/September 2002.

Clarence Page — "Church Needs to Provide Moral Clarity," *Liberal Opinion Week,* May 6, 2002.

Margot Patterson — "Priests Question Fairness of Policy," *National Catholic Reporter,* July 5, 2002.

Leon J. Podles — "Catholic Scandals: A Crisis for Celibacy?" *Touchstone,* March 28, 2002.

Pat Power — "Catholic Church Must Confront Issue of Celibacy," *TheAge.com,* August 29, 2002.

John R. Quinn — "Considerations for a Church in Crisis," *America,* May 27, 2002.

Charley Reese — "Child Abusers Deserve No Break," *Conservative Chronicle,* July 31, 2002.

Rosemary Radford Ruether — "Abuse a Consequence of Historic Wrong Turn: Priesthood and Celibacy Need to Be Distinct Vocations Once Again," *National Catholic Reporter,* June 7, 2002.

Marianne Szegedy-Maszak, Michael Schaffer, and Dan Gilgoff — "Chastity and Lust," *U.S. News & World Report,* April 1, 2002.

Rembert Weakland — "Long- and Short-Term Goals in Addressing Clergy Sexual Abuse," *Origins,* May 16, 2002.

Carol Zaleski — "In Defense of Celibacy," *The Christian Century,* May 8, 2002.

Websites

ABC News — "'Bless Me Father for I Have Sinned': The Catholic Church in Crisis." *abcNEWS.com.* Website includes news, interviews, commentary, and links to resources for victims, clergy, and Catholic laity. www.abcnews.go.com/onair/DailyNews/pjr020403_ChurchCrisis_sub.html.

Boston Globe — *Spotlight Investigation: Abuse in the Catholic Church.* Website includes a chronology of the child sexual abuse scandal, current and past news coverage, commentary, depositions, and the reactions of victims, priests, and Catholic laity. www.boston.com/globe/spotlight/abuse.

United States Conference of Catholic Bishops — *Restoring Trust: A Response to Clergy Sexual Abuse.* Website includes history, policy, remarks, statements, presentations, and the Charter for the Protection of Children and Young People. www.usccb.org/comm/restoretrust.htm.

Index

abusers
  actions taken against
    defrocking of, 10, 14
    lenient nature of, 9, 10
    reassignment of, 9
    suspension of, 83
  compassion for, 91
  lack of data about, 41
  majority are ephebephiles, 58–59
  most were molested as minors, 42
  multiple molestations by, 9, 10, 14, 39, 69
  number of
    accused, 76
    estimated, 41, 56
  stunted emotional growth of, 41
accountability, 46, 51, 62, 66, 88
Ad Majorem Dei Gloriam (magazine), 82
American Psychiatric Association, 68, 72
Australia, 11
Austria, 11

Beaudoin, Tom, 52
Bellavance, David, 79
Berlin, Frederick, 17–19, 21, 39, 70, 71
Bernardin, Joseph, 92
Bertone, Tarcisio, 61
Bevilacqua, Anthony, 70
Birmingham, Joseph, 14
bishops. *See* Catholic Church, hierarchy of
blackmail, 61
Boston Globe (newspaper), 9, 12, 14, 69, 76
boys. *See* ephebephilia; pedophilia
Brady, Stephen, 82
Braine, John, 35–36
Burns, John F., 69

Canada, 11
Catholic Church
  celibacy in
    attracts homosexuals, 20, 26
    attracts men with sexual problems, 40
    Catholic Church definition of, 70
    chastity and, 29
    contributes to sexual abuse, 19
    con, 18, 34, 40
    contributes to shortage of priests, 18
    development of, 29, 32–33
    enables better performance of

      pastoral duties, 19, 33
    enhances dependency of priests
      upon hierarchy, 30
    fosters culture of secrecy, 18
    heterosexuals and, 26
    is not immutable, 11, 33, 34
    is not related to pedophilia, 19, 28, 34
    is related to ephebephilia, 19
    perception of, by priests, 29
    popular view of, 31–32
  culture of secrecy in
    blackmail and, 61
    celibacy fosters, 18
    harms Catholic Church, 49
    is used to protect image of Catholic Church, 65
    leads to distrust of hierarchy, 46
  hierarchy of
    accountability of, 46, 62, 66
    acted in good faith, 16, 23
      failed to understand seriousness of molestations, 11
    were given poor advice, 92
    apologies by, 14
    civil authorities deferred to, 17
    compassion for, 92
    concerns of
      fiscal solvency, 83
      limiting legal liability, 12
      protection of image, 12, 36–37, 50–51, 65
    cover-ups were response of, 9, 17
    con, 9, 15, 23
    criminal prosecution requires cooperation of, 26, 81
    culture of secrecy and, 46, 49, 65
    dependence of priests on, 30
    false accusations of molestation against, 92
    financial irresponsibility of, 79, 80
    homosexuals in, 60–61, 82–83
    illicit sex by, 80, 81
    inaction by, 14
    laity and
      accountability to, 46, 66
      anger of, 15, 42
    molestations and
      blamed society for, 12
      blamed victims, 10
      viewed as failure of moral

103

Novak, Michael, 61–62

O'Neill, Thomas P., Jr., 12
Opus Dei, 20

Paetz, Julius, 16
parochial schools, 76, 77, 78, 80
pastoral confidentiality, 43–44
pederasty, 71–72, 73
pedophilia/pedophiles
  can be cured, 39, 71
    con, 17
  celibacy is not related to, 19, 28, 34
  differ greatly, 39, 40
  homosexuals as, 20, 21
  is not always harmful, 72
  is not related to homosexuality, 42
  as mental illness, 68, 72, 75
  moral responsibility of, 74
Perez-Calixto, Lucila, 77
Peterson, Michael R., 11
Pilot, The (official publication of
  Archdiocese of Boston), 41
Pius X, 65
Poland, 16
Pope, Stephen J., 48
Porter, James, 44–45
priests
  abuse of, in seminaries, 16
  bisexual, 20
  defrocking of, 44–45
    Geoghan, 76
    Kos, 76
    opposes teaching of Catholic
      Church, 64
    zero-tolerance policy does not
      require, 53, 56
  dependency on hierarchy of, 30
  dying of AIDS, 81
  extent of sexual activity among, 11,
    20–21
    consensual, 80
  false accusations of molestation
    against, 92
  homosexual
    in hierarchy, 60–61, 82–83
    many deny their sexuality, 21
    ordination of
      is discouraged by Vatican, 61–62
      should be prohibited, 19–20, 26
      should not be prohibited, 42
    percentage of, 20–21, 34, 59–60
    power of, 60
    on seminary faculties, 62
  married, 16, 33, 34, 59
  maturity level at ordination of, 29, 30
  percentage who are abusers, 41
  perception of celibacy by, 29
  power of, 26, 37

shame of nonabusing, 81, 90–91, 92
shortage of, 16
  celibacy contributes to, 18
  women as, 16, 59
  see also abusers
"Problem of Sexual Molestation by
  Roman Catholic Clergy: Meeting the
  Problem in a Comprehensive and
  Responsible Manner" (Mouton, Doyle,
  and Peterson), 11
prodigal son, 67
Psychological Bulletin (journal), 72
Psychopathia Sexualis (Krafft-Ebing), 72

rehabilitation, 39–40
Rehkemper, Robert, 79
repentance, 11, 26
responsibility. *See* moral responsibility
Rind, Bruce, 72
Roman Catholic Faithful, Inc. (RCF), 82
Rooney, Don, 9
Rose, Michael S., 60
Rossetti, Stephen J., 17, 18, 19, 38
Rubino, Stephen, 58–59, 61
Rusher, William, 24
Russell, Bertrand, 35
Ruygt, Hans, 81
Ryan, Daniel, 82–83

Schoener, Gary, 17, 19
self-sacrifice, 33
seminaries
  abuse of priests in, 16
  authentically Catholic ones are filled,
    63
  closing of, 77, 81
  homosexuals on faculties of, 62
  improved screening of candidates for,
    19
  sexual activity in, 21, 60
service, philosophy of, 65
settlements
  cost of, 9, 15, 75–76, 78–80, 82, 88
  gag orders in, 43, 83
  secrecy of, 65
Sexual Healing Journey, The (Maltz), 87
Shanley, Paul, 13–14, 49
Shaughnessy, Paul, 63
sin
  compassion and, 91
  differences in severity of, 53
  homosexuality as, 61, 79
  molestation as, 23, 69
  of omission, 50
  repentance and, 26
Sipe, Richard, 19, 20, 59, 60, 62
society
  frequency of child sexual abuse in,
    41–42